The Woodturner's Companion

The Woodturner's Companion

Ron Roszkiewicz

with the collaboration of
Phyllis Straw

 Sterling Publishing Co. Inc. New York
Distributed in the U.K. by Blandford Press

EDITED BY KATHERINE BALCH

Library of Congress Cataloging in Publication Data
Roszkiewicz, Ron.
  The woodturner's companion.

  Includes index.
  1. Turning. I. Straw, Phyllis. II. Title.
TT201.R67 1984   684'.083   84-8557
ISBN 0-8069-7940-2 (pbk.)

Published by Sterling Publishing Co., Inc.
Two Park Avenue, New York, N.Y. 10016
Distributed in Australia by Oak Tree Press Co., Ltd.
P.O. Box K514 Haymarket, Sydney 2000, N.S.W.
Distributed in the United Kingdom by Blandford Press
Link House, West Street, Poole, Dorset BH15 ILL, England
Distributed in Canada by Oak Tree Press Ltd.
% Canadian Manda Group, P.O. Box 920, Station U
Toronto, Ontario, Canada M8Z 5P9
Manufactured in the United States of America

This book is dedicated to Adam.

Table of Contents

PREFACE

Most woodturners that I have come in contact with are of the home-taught variety and will usually admit to proceeding very, very slowly with their technical growth. Translating into written form the action of and reaction to advancing tools into a spinning, exposed piece of wood seems to me more difficult to explain than, say, cutting a finger joint on a table saw. The variables—wood, speed, sharpened bevels, and positions of hands—seem so great, and the fear factor, enhanced by the first misstep, is so strong that skew chisels become scrapers and cutting tools are often underused.

So this is my shot at demystifying woodturning. My experience ranges from putting a spindle on a lathe, switching it on, and jumping back to see what would happen, to teaching people to rough out a square billet with one skew and turn a bowl with one gouge. I had help along the way. Friendships and both formal and informal instruction from Peter Child, John Sainsbury, Dale Nish, and Bob Stocksdale exposed me to the broad range of possibilities for working cleanly and quickly. My technique is a blend of their styles and my own, discovered through experiment.

The key will always be practice. Understand the basic principles first and practice without cluttering up the effort with design. Reducing a cord of wood to thick luxurious shavings in order to master the skew chisel brings the unique gratification that only mastery of a technique can provide. I've done my best to define every conceivable aspect of the process, and I hope that my techniques will inspire confidence in others, so they will be free to enjoy the art of woodturning—a celebration of the beauty of wood.

ACKNOWLEDGMENTS

Over the past ten years woodworkers have become more generous with their information and experience. I was fortunate as catalogue director for the Woodcraft Supply Corp. to be exposed to this wealth of information and innovation, and I wish to thank the following people for their assistance in my development: Mark Perry, Peter Child, Albert LeCoff, David Ellsworth, David Powell, John Tierney, Paul Chase, Dick Dabrowski, Gerry McIntosh, John Sainsbury, Michael Germer, Bob Stocksdale, and Tage Frid.

My wife, Phyllis, and I shared a unique experience in developing this book. The many words and pictures that marked the eventual outcome were the result of two years of our talking, thinking, writing, and revising. Although the process threatened to completely upset our lives, it was, in the end, an important part of our growth. I also thank my parents, Rudolph and Jeannette Roszkiewicz, for their help.

At Sterling Publishing Co. I wish to thank Charlie Nurnberg for sponsoring the book and Katherine Balch for her excellent work editing it.

The
Woodturner's
Companion

I · The Woodturning Tradition

*I*n attempting to compile a comprehensive history of wood-turning, the historian is continually confronted with one major obstacle—the inevitable perishability of wood. Unlike metals and earthenware, wooden articles, particularly those used as common utensils, are short-lived, disappearing without a trace. We have evidence for the evolution of the lathe, and it is possible to examine the relative importance of wood to humankind's cultural ascent. But my preference is to treat the historical aspects of turning by considering the craft as an ongoing process and by reviewing the basic kinds of objects produced. Most existing examples of turned objects were made within the last 400 years, an extremely fertile time for craft production, and most included here are drawn from British and Colonial American craftwork. For my purposes, three categories—turned common ware, ceremonial and high-style turned objects, and ornamental turned objects—will serve as a brief look into the past.

Turned Common Ware

Wood is a readily available material and easy to fashion into the utensils required of everyday life. For this reason, we find that through the centuries people have relied on wood for shelter and fuel and for many of the instruments and vessels used in domestic and work settings. The common ware used in everyday life has often been purely functional. The rigors of both the roughhewn English agrarian life and the American pioneering life left little time for decoration of common ware, and when it does appear in artifacts, it is simple—a groove, a rounded edge, or some other subtle refinement. Although regional styles and traditions are apparent, most simple utensils were thick and made of native woods that were easily turned fresh from the log. Woods such as birch, beech, and sycamore were favored because they added no flavor of their own to the substance they held. Furniture items, from simple milking stools to elegant chairs (Illus. 1–3), were also made from native woods and decorated simply with colorful paints or stains.

2

3

Most turned common ware was produced by craft specialists who might have produced bowls, plates (Illus. 4), and scoops (Illus. 5) as part of a broader line of vessels for holding wet or dry goods. However, it was not unusual for farmers to fashion turned legs in quantity for sale to furniture makers or to make household items for their own use on a simple lathe housed in the barn. In England, a special group of itinerant turners known as bodgers emerged to satisfy the steady need for gross upon gross of identically turned legs for Windsor chairs. The legs were sold to shops that produced and assembled the other necessary parts of the chair. Setting up a hut among the trees and devising a spring-pole lathe using a nearby sapling, the bodger processed previously felled logs into quantities of spindles. He was an independent sort who combined speed and accuracy to maintain his reputation.

Illus. 2. Slat back chair (Delaware Valley, 1730–1850, walnut, H.: 45 in., W. at seat: 18½ in., 62.1190, Gift of Mrs. Charles Russell Codman. Courtesy, Museum of Fine Arts, Boston).

Illus. 3. Carver armchair (American, 17th century, ash, H.: 1.06m, 32.225, Bequest of Charles Hitchcock Tyler. Courtesy, Museum of Fine Arts, Boston).

Illus. 4. Selection of plates: left, *walnut;* above right, *myrtle burl;* and below right, *oak.*

Illus. 5. Mass-produced common ware made on an automatic lathe.

4

5

More than any other form of turning, common ware puts us in touch with the people who used it. Plates with knife marks from cutting meat and bleached white from scouring evoke much of the feeling and life-style of the times. Chairs, worn and coated with wax and wood-fire soot, show the honest patination of generations of use.

Ceremonial and High-Style Turned Objects

Precious objects have always required special containers to hold them, and during the last 400 years the patronage of the aristocracy and clergy made possible the development of a rich tradition in ceremonial and high-style turned objects. Substances we take for granted today held special and often mysterious positions in the past either because they were expensive and difficult to obtain or because they represented integral parts of primitive rituals or religious or state ceremonies. The most highly skilled craftsmen and the most exotic materials were employed to produce these special pieces; a ceremonial goblet turned in ebony, for instance, would have been ornamented by a carver and inlaid with precious metals by a goldsmith. Exquisite turnings, carved and gilded, were also needed for ceremonial thrones (Illus. 6). The lavish homes of the English aristocracy featured the refined design elements found in ceremonial vessels and containers. Extra time and skill were needed to produce the delicate turnings for a tilt-top table (Illus. 7), plant stand (Illus. 8), or stair-

Illus. 6. "Thrown" chair (English, 17th century, oak, H.: 1.23 m, 32.228, Bequest of Charles Hitchcock Tyler. Courtesy, Museum of Fine Arts, Boston).

Illus. 7. Chippendale tea table (American, Philadelphia, 1760–1775, mahogany, H.: 2 ft. 5⅞ in., scalloped and tilting top, 39.146, Gift of Mr. and Mrs. Maxim Karolik. Courtesy, Museum of Fine Arts, Boston).

6   7

Illus. 8. Urn stand (attrib. to Samuel McIntire, American, ca. 1795, mahogany, H.: 2 ft. 6 in., D.: top 11½ in., 23.34, M. and M. Karolik Collection. Courtesy, Museum of Fine Arts, Boston).

Illus. 9. Press cupboard (attrib. to Thomas Denni, working 1688 d. 1706, American, Ipswich, Mass., oak and pine, W.: 48½ in., H.: 58¾ in., Depth.: 19⅜ in., 51.53, Gift of Maurice Geeraerts in memory of Mr. and Mrs. William H. Robeson. Courtesy, Museum of Fine Arts, Boston).

case balustrade. These expensive items were manufactured by shops that specialized in current urban trends or that worked closely with architects in executing their designs. The precious linen and dishes treasured by Britons and colonists alike were housed in chests with turnings split in half and applied (Illus. 9). These were often ebonized to simulate rare ebony wood.

Obviously, the balance of form and function is nearly equal in ceremonial and high-style turning (Illus. 10). Although decorated chests or yuletide wassail bowls were designed primarily to hold objects or liquids, the weight given to aesthetic considerations in design created a special ceremonial air and enhanced the occasions associated with their use.

8

9

Illus. 10. Four post bed (Boston or Salem, ca. 1808, mahogany, pine and oak, H.: 221.9 cm, 23.12, Gift of Martha C. Codman. Courtesy, Museum of Fine Arts, Boston).

Ornamental Turned Objects

Until the publication of *L'Art de Tourner* (The Art of Turning) by the French botanist Charles Plumier (1646–1704) in 1701, ornamental turning was probably the domain of a very small group of master craftsmen. Plumier popularized woodturning by documenting the craft and detailing the construction of simple and complex lathes. The hobby of ornamental turning became a widespread pastime among the European aristocracy and undoubtedly led in 18th-century England to John Jacob Holtzapffel (1768–1835) (Illus. 11) manufacturing the ornamental turning lathe (Illus. 12). Prior to this time, lathes were were spare in design and not the subjects of prideful ownership associated with the aristocracy. Extra care and decorative machining (Illus. 13) made the Holtzapffel lathe worth its 1500 pound (sterling) price. A complete and custom-made setup—including the Rose Engine Lathe, geometric and ellipse chucks, cutters and sharpeners, and hand-turning tools—equalled about 10,000 dollars at the time. Although the market was limited, Holtzapffel produced 2557 machines.

Cost-effectiveness and marketability were not considerations in the execution on this machine of often beautiful, always enchanting designs (Illus. 14). It was capable of making any cut to produce any effect. The step-by-step process, which had to be devised before the

Illus. 11. John Jacob Holtzapffel (1768–1835) was an Alsatian mechanic who settled in London in 1794 and built his first lathe in the following year.

Illus. 12. Holtzapffel Rose Engine Lathe No. 1636. Holtzapffel considered this lathe, made between 1836 and 1838 for John Taylor, Esq., to be the finest Rose Engine Lathe ever crafted by his firm. The lathe and the accompanying complete and original set of accessories (Illus. 13a–i) are now in the collection of Warren Greene Ogden, Jr.

13a

13b

13c

13d

Illus. 13a. Headstock of the Rose Engine Lathe. Each bronze rosette in the assembly constitutes a separate pattern. The guide bar along the front holds a rubber that follows the pattern chosen by the lathe operator.

Illus. 13b. Ellipse chuck attached to the headstock is capable of making a perfect ellipse in any kind of wood or nonferrous metal.

Illus. 13c. The business end of the Holtzapffel Rose Engine Lathe consists of the slide rest, geometric chuck, and headstock.

Illus. 13d. Infinitely variable rotation sequences can be present for this geometric chuck.

13f

13e

13f

Illus. 13f. The slide rest contains cutter bits that move independently of the headstock and chuck. Detail shows a cutting bit and the pulleys around which a cord is wrapped to activate the cutter assembly according to a preset speed and sequence of movement.

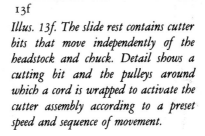

13e

Illus. 13e. The geometric chuck consists of three parts that can be individually set. Detail shows a pencil pattern that reflects the setting of the chuck.

Illus. 13g. These highly decorated dividers were used for ornamental turning.

13g

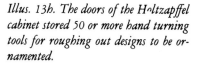

Illus. 13h. The doors of the Holtzapffel cabinet stored 50 or more hand turning tools for roughing out designs to be ornamented.

13h

Illus. 13i. This custom-fit mahogany cabinet, which held all the necessary chucks and accessories, accompanied each Holtzapffel lathe.

13i

14b

14a

Illus. 14a. Gold box (property of Patty Earle Ogden) decorated on Rose Engine Lathe.

Illus. 14b. This tortoiseshell box was cut with an ellipse chuck mounted on the Rose Engine Lathe.

first cut could be made, was in fact an intellectual exercise requiring some degree of engineering and mathematical ability. The end result could take as long as six months to achieve. The materials used were ebony, kingwood, ivory, tortoiseshell, and other exotic, dense, machinable mediums. The designs mimicked carved motifs with the sharp-edged precision we take for granted today. As a one-of-a-kind hobby, ornamental turning is similar to recent craftwork.

Certainly, the balance of form and function shifts almost completely to form and process in the practice of ornamental turning. Although hardly widespread any longer, it is still alive today and held together by correspondence within the Society of Ornamental Turners. The society's leading bibliographer knows the history of all 2557 Holtzapffel lathes and notes that little work of any significance seems to be performed on them today.

14c

14d

14e

14f

Illus. 14c. This exotic wood box was made with a geometric chuck and a diamond cutting tool for superb finish.

Illus. 14d. The lids of these exotic wood boxes were cut using the Rose Engine Lathe.

Illus. 14e. Exercise pieces made of exotic woods and ivory show a few of the many cuts possible on an ornamental turning lathe.

Illus. 14f. This ivory sphere within a sphere was made on a hand-turning lathe by following chucking procedures common to ornamental turning and described in Hand or Simple Turning by John Jacob Holtzapffel.

A Case History: the Tools of J. F. Rondeau

The end of the 19th century was an active period for woodturning in the United States. Victorian styles routinely included turned ornamentation for furniture, architecture (Illus. 15–17), and decorative accessories. J. F. Rondeau, who lived in central Massachusetts, was a unique spindle turner of this time, producing everything from small finials (Illus. 18) to large architectural columns (Illus. 19). He also collected turning tools and experimented with their design. I bought the collection from his son who had stored them for over 50 years.

15a

15b

15c

Illus. 15a–c. Turned columns and spindles typical of the Victorian era.

16a

16b

Illus. 16a–c. Turned and subsequently carved spindles.

16c

His chest includes over 75 tools (Illus. 20) and five calipers (Illus. 21). The gouges (Illus. 22) range in size—that is, the size of the corresponding cove that the tool can cut—from very fine to extremely large (Illus. 23). Most of the handles (Illus. 24) in this collection are workman-made birch and correspond in length and diameter to the mass of the blades. All of the blades are well finished with exact and well-shaped profiles (Illus. 25 and 26). Included in the collection are six rosewood-handled tools, which he purchased from a retiring turner. Although such a purchase was common practice among craftsmen, he admonished his son against it and asked that his tools be stored away after his death. The inclusion of the huge Lancastershire-pattern calipers with the smaller sizes attests to the breadth of his professional activity. The calipers are beautifully balanced by gentle tapers in the thickness of the legs. The tool chest in which the tools came is typical of a turner who may have hired himself out and needed a portable chest for his tools.

Rondeau tried to perfect the parting tool. What he wanted was a tool that would cut quickly and shear across the long-grain fibres on a spindle, leaving a smooth shoulder free of tearing. He succeeded, and Illus. 27 shows the results. (In the spindle turning section I de-

17

17

Illus. 17. A roof-top gallery composed of split turnings.

Illus. 18a–c. Turned and subsequently carved finials.

Illus. 19. Columns turned and reeded with a hand plane.

18a   18b   18c

19

Illus. 20a,b. The chest and tools of J. F. Rondeau. Over 75 tools were packed into this well-made and portable chest.

Illus. 21a,b. These examples of Rondeau's calipers were well balanced and represent pieces of delicately wrought metal craftsmanship.

Illus. 22. Most professional craftsmen are also tool collectors. Duplication is practical because it means more work can be accomplished between sharpenings.

Illus. 23. Gouge sizes in Rondeau's collection range from very fine to extremely large.

20a

20b

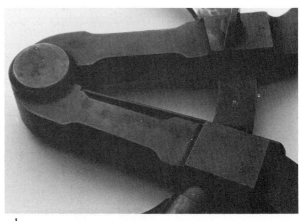

21a

21b

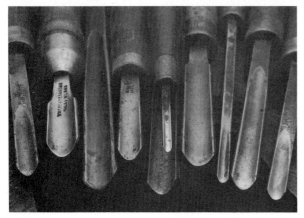

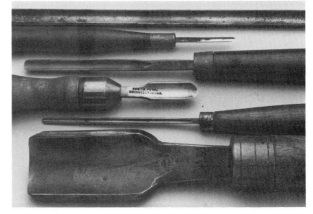

22

23

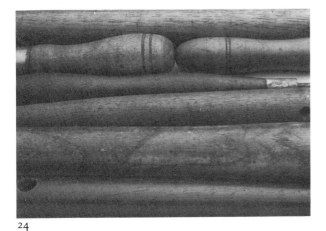

24

25a

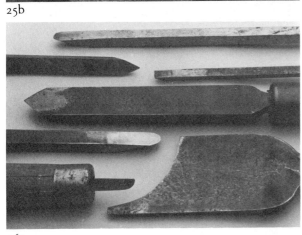

25b

25c

26a

26b

Illus. 24. Rondeau's handmade handles. It was common at that time for turners to buy blades and then make their own handles out of ordinary woods.

Illus. 25a–c. A selection of beautifully forged chisels from Rondeau's chest. The grinding of corners and the rounding over of edges are typical of tool modifications made by turners to enhance movement along the tool rest.

Illus. 26a,b. Rondeau's scrapers. Each shape was ground by Rondeau from steel blanks to accommodate a routine or a special job.

scribe the advantages and disadvantages of the various parting-tool styles.) This tool was the precursor of the modern hollow-ground design. J. F. Rondeau died in 1900 before his handwork could become obsolete in the modern industrialized age. But I believe that if he were alive today, he would still respond to the needs of his time by producing furniture and architectural elements with exquisite turnings. His tools tell not only of his versatility but also of his appreciation of fine workmanship.

Woodturning Today

Examples of mass-produced and disposable turned objects are commonplace. Thread reels, pepper grinders, and furniture legs owe their

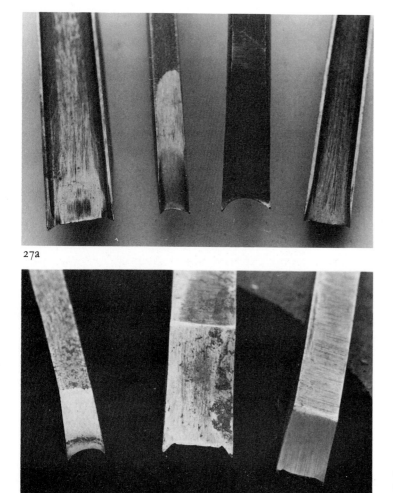

27a

27b

Illus. 27a,b. Examples of Rondeau's experimentation with the perfect parting tool.

shapes to tradition, the knife grinder, and the automatic lathe. There was never any romance in making them, and they are best made by machine. However, automation unfortunately caused a direct break in the pursuit of the craft of woodturning, and techniques were lost. Few masters remain to pass on the skills that form the foundation for the creative development of the craft. Woodturners today learn from books as did the aristocratic readers of Plumier. But even the best authors find that the subtleties of the craft are difficult to describe. Perhaps a current picture of woodturning can be drawn by defining the sources of modern turned objects.

Turned common ware. Automatic lathes produce quantities of simple turnings, more decorated than the common ware of the past, but still simple when compared with the high-style or ornamental categories. The woods used are maple and birch because of their availability, plain grain, ability to absorb stains evenly, and ability to hold some detail. Machined wooden plates and goblets are not practical for everyday use because of the availability of inexpensive and more durable plastics and ceramics. But coat pegs, pepper grinders, and other accessories have a ready market thanks to the current nostalgia for country life and the pleasing nature of the wood itself. Most hobbyists produce common ware as they discover the techniques of the past. Toys, clocks, bowls, and simple colonial-style furniture are items most often produced.

Ceremonial and high-style turned objects. Advanced amateur and professional turners produce items that fall into this category. Simple forms and exotic woods executed with delicacy and elegance are the hallmarks of fine turnings today. Containers and vessels finished with clear matt oils and varnishes show off the marble and gemlike qualities of burls, tropical hardwoods, and highly figured domestic woods. Each piece is unique and treated with ceremony by the eventual owner. These pieces are visual statements for the turner and the owner. Their display in homes built and furnished with the products of mass production lends a sort of balance to a contemporary interior.

Current high-style furniture, when it does employ turned elements, is almost always strongly derivative of the past (Illus. 28–35), or an outright reproduction. The boundaries have barely begun to be stretched.

28a

28b

29

Illus. 28a,b. Built-up container made of bird's-eye maple and rosewood, by Ron Roszkiewicz.

Illus. 29. Built-up container made of boxwood and rosewood, by Ron Roszkiewicz.

Illus. 30. Hourglass made of mahogany and white oak, by Ron Roszkiewicz.

30

31

32

33a

33b

Illus. 31. Mahogany bowl by Ron Roszkiewicz.

Illus. 32. Claro walnut bowl with rose-wood inlay, by Ron Roszkiewicz.

Illus. 33a,b. Built-up container made of red maple burl and ebony, by Ron Roszkiewicz.

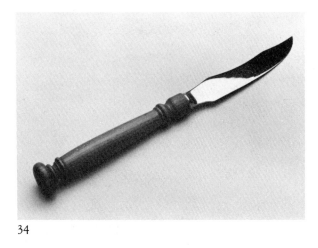

34   35

A new branch of high-style turning has developed. Nonfunctional
sculpture made of exotic and figured woods has entered the fine arts
marketplace (Illus. 36). Because the wood itself is the principal or-
nament, the technical skill of the turner must be matched with equal
sensitivity to the inherent beauty of the wood. Simplicity of line and
proportion is currently popular and is used to expose the exotic nature of the wood without obstructing it with a great deal of detailing. This branch of the craft is new but will no doubt continue to
develop, subject to more visibility in the marketplace and increased
popularity among collectors.

Ornamental turned objects. Many of the original ornamental
turning lathes are still in existence and continue to be used, but to a
more limited extent than in the past. The British Society of Ornamental Turners is the current forum where owners of these lathes
exchange both historical and technical information. It is still an aristocratic hobby practiced by modern-day technocratic engineering ge-
niuses. (See Illus. 37 and 38.)

The Future of Woodturning

The slow discovery of past techniques and the limited use of turnings in contemporary sculptural and furniture forms continue to
delay the progress of the craft. There are signs of the creative use of
turnings as sculptural elements in both simple and complex designs
(Illus. 39–40). The forms of these turnings are derivative but in the

*Illus. 34. Tulipwood knife handle by
Ron Roszkiewicz.*

*Illus. 35. Rattle made of boxwood, by
Ron Roszkiewicz.*

*Illus. 36. Nonfunctional turned sculp-
ture made of sugar maple burl. No. 11
in the series* Man and the Forest Architecture, *by David Ellsworth (7 x
15½ in.).*

37b

Illus. 37a,b. Built-up threaded container made of boxwood in 18th-century French style, by M. U. Zakariya.

37a

38b

Illus. 38a,b. Built-up threaded container made of cherry in 18th-century French style, by M. U. Zakariya.

38a

context of each piece they provide excitement as they lend symmetry or asymmetry to the total design. In many cases the lathe is used only as a machine to mill simple round shapes. This use of the lathe, especially in light of the contemporary wealth of turning experience and possibilities, does not provide new stimulus for growth.

The field of woodworking is more open today than ever before. Experimentation is prevalent in the use of more exotic materials, in state-of-the-art paints, stains, and surface treatments, and in carved details drawn from contemporary historical perspectives. Woodturning as an allied art to the larger category of woodworking will continue to grow. Because wood is a popular medium today, many of the experiments in wood are encouraged and subsidized. It will only be a matter of time before we recognize a new golden age of woodturning. Signs that it has begun are already here.

Illustrated on the following pages are examples of what some master turners are now producing (Illus. 41–48).

Illus. 39. Chair with polychromed and gilded turned legs, by Wendell Castle.

Illus. 40. Desk and credenza with polychromed and gilded turned legs, by Wendell Castle.

40

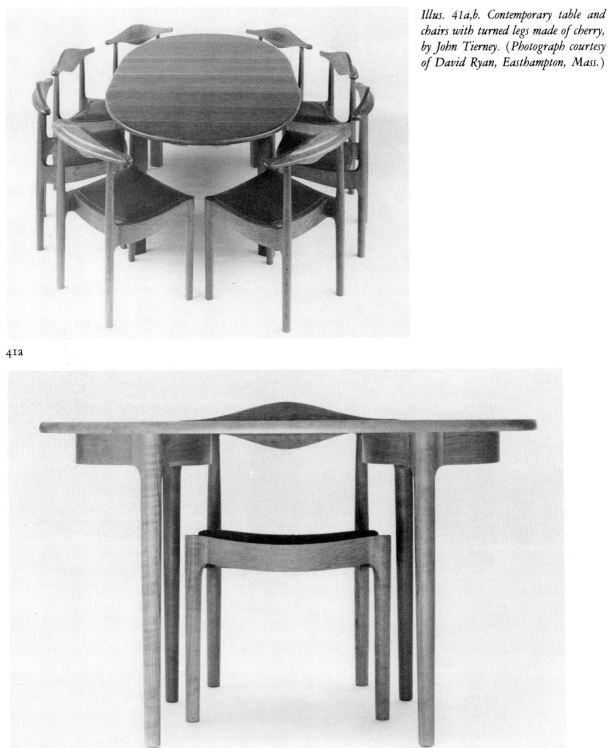

Illus. 41a,b. Contemporary table and chairs with turned legs made of cherry, by John Tierney. (Photograph courtesy of David Ryan, Easthampton, Mass.)

41a

41b

43

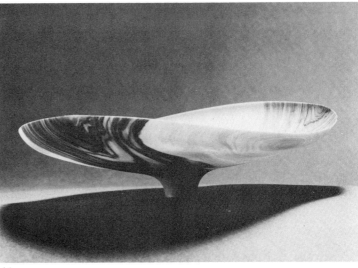

44

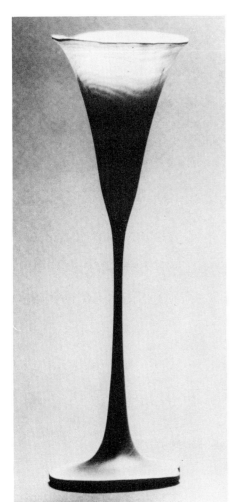

42

Illus. 42. Manzanita, translucent goblet, 8 in. tall, 0.014 in. thick, by Del Stubbs.

Illus. 43. Pistachio, translucent bowl, 7 in. diameter, 0.018 in. thick, by Del Stubbs.

Illus. 44. Olive bowl, 7 in. diameter, 0.015 in. thick, by Del Stubbs.

Illus. 45. Bowl made from kou, a Hawaiian wood, 12½ in. diameter, 6 in. tall, by Bob Stocksdale.

Illus. 46. Bowl made from thuya burl, a Moroccan wood, 5½ in. diameter, 6 in. tall, by Bob Stocksdale.

Illus. 47. Almond, translucent bowl, 8 in. diameter, 0.018 in. thick, by Del Stubbs.

45

46

47

Illus. 48. A series of nested eggs made of (from largest to smallest) tulip-wood, ironwood, lignum vitae, bone, and ebony, and also a goblet made of boxwood. A chicken egg and an ant are included to show relative size. The photograph enlarges these objects by 385%. (Photograph courtesy of Paul Atkins, Chico, Calif.)

II · The Turner's Shop

*W*oodturning does not require a lot of space, but there are some layout considerations that will make the work area safer and the ancillary tools accessible. In the turner's shop the lathe is the focus of activity. The lathe is also one of many machines used in the production of a piece of furniture. In most of the cabinet-making shops that I have seen the lathe is positioned off in a corner or against the wall. This location is claustrophobic for me, and I have always moved my lathe out into the middle of the room.

I also like to get as much natural light as possible. Of course in some shops after the central locations have been filled with table saw, jointer, and planer, there is little space remaining for another tool. In that case a window location can open things up a bit. No matter where you place the lathe some sort of artificial lighting will be needed. I prefer incandescent light over fluorescent light and use a flexible-arm, graphic arts type of lamp (Illus. 49) so that I can position it wherever I need it most. This is perfect for looking inside a bowl or seeing the shadows on the top of a spindle. Fluorescent lights wash out shadows and fill every crevice of a turning with light and actually make it more difficult to judge sizes and shapes.

The floor material around the lathe must be resilient. Carpeting reduces the fatigue of long hours at the machine and softens the blow for falling tools and bowls. When I began turning I tried to reduce fatigue even further by turning while perched on a tall stool. My legs were fine after that first session, but my shoulder and arm were strained by the new position. Because I use my entire body, I try as much as possible to distribute the stress.

The other tools that I use, my tool chest, and workbench have all evolved into a semicircle around me. With only a half-turn I can reach my tool chest, two steps get me to my sharpening system, and one-and-one-half steps put me in front of my workbench. This convenience is achieved without sacrificing the safe open space around my lathe. I can work on a motor or clean up the mess without being an acrobat.

Anatomy of the Lathe

A discussion of the turner's shop appropriately begins with the anatomy of the lathe (Illus. 50). The principal parts that make up the lathe are: the headstock, lathe bed, tailstock, tool rest, tool-rest base, stand, and motor. Even with seven major components, the lathe is a very simple device.

The headstock is the business end of the machine and is usually made of a heavy cast-iron or aluminum casting (Illus. 51). This casting encases the cylindrical, machined spindle, which is most often threaded at both ends and hollow through the middle. Work-holding devices are held on the threaded ends of this spindle. Part of the spindle assembly is the pulley. The most common pulley type is the 4-step pulley (Illus. 52), which is shaped like a cone with four distinct grooved steps along its length. A matching pulley is mounted on the motor and joined to the headstock by a V-belt. The diameters of the steps on the motor pulley run in the opposite direction from the steps on the headstock pulley. The four steps correspond to four speeds without any overlap. Also encased in the headstock is a pair of ball bearings sealed in lubricant. They surround the spindle and facilitate its movement. In most cases the headstock is bolted to the lathe; for some special operations it can be unbolted, and a spacer block can be inserted between it and the lathe. This allows for larger turnings to be mounted over the bed of the lathe. The only additional gear needed is a longer V-belt and longer bolts.

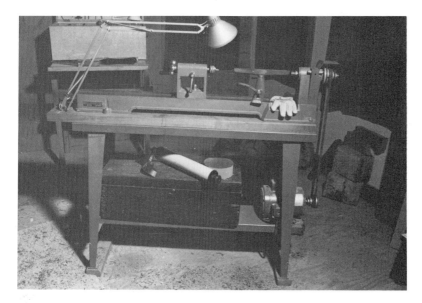

Illus. 50. Lathe.

51

52

Illus. 51. Headstock with threaded spindle. Work-holding devices are threaded onto or held within the cylindrical machined spindle.

Illus. 52. A 4-step pulley on the headstock spindle assembly.

The long flat surface that makes up the length of the lathe is called the bed or ways (Illus. 53). The headstock is bolted to the bed. The bed is commonly made of cast iron, round seamless steel tubing, sheet steel bent into a box shape, or heavy wood beams. The important part of the bed is the working surface, on which the movable lathe parts slide. It must be straight and smooth. The heavy, bed materials not only absorb the vibration during the turning process but also maintain the accuracy of the bed. The capacity of a lathe, or the sizes of wood it can accommodate, is determined by the distance between the headstock and tailstock and also by the radius from the center point of the headstock spindle to the bed. The latter is called the swing, and it is half the diameter of the largest disc that can be mounted on the spindle. Some lathes have a depression at the headstock end (Illus. 54) to increase the capacity of the lathe. These are called gap-bed lathes. The swing of most lathes seems to range from 10 to 12 in. (25.4 to 30.5 cm). Bed lengths usually run from 36 to 42 in. (91.4 to 106.7 cm). For larger turnings the other side of the headstock is used. If larger spindles are needed, it is both possible and practical to join together smaller spindles after turning with a socket-and-tenon joint.

The tailstock (Illus. 55) is the movable end of the lathe opposite the headstock. It usually has a hollow spindle, a handwheel for advancing the spindle, and a locking nut for tightening the spindle in position. Another locking-nut assembly tightens the tailstock onto the lathe bed at any position along its length. The hollow spindle (Illus. 56) can hold a ball-bearing center for supporting the opposite end of a wooden blank or for holding a drill chuck for drilling wood held on the headstock.

The tool rest (Illus. 57 and 58) supports the blade of the tool during cutting or scraping. It can be adjusted up or down and piv-

Illus. 53. Lathe bed.

Illus. 54. Lathe bed gap forms a depression at the headstock end to increase the lathe's capacity.

Illus. 55. The tailstock includes, from the left, the hand wheel for advancing the spindle, a locking nut for tightening the spindle in position, another locking-nut assembly to tighten the tailstock onto the lathe bed, and a hollow spindle to hold dead and ball-bearing centers to support the opposite end of a wooden blank.

Illus. 56. A close-up view of the tailstock spindle shows the hollow for holding centers and the machined increments used when drilling with the tailstock.

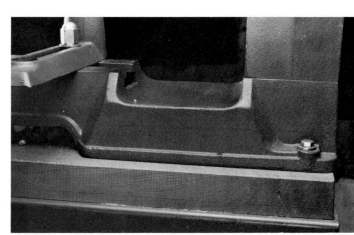

53

54

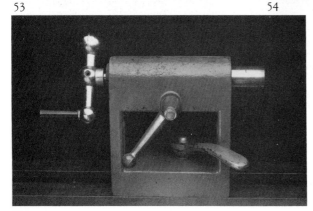

55

56

Illus. 57. Three sizes of straight tool rests used in spindle turning include: (a) 3 in. (76 mm), (b) 12 in. (30.5 cm), and (c) 24 in. (61 cm). The tool-rest base holds each in position on the lathe bed.

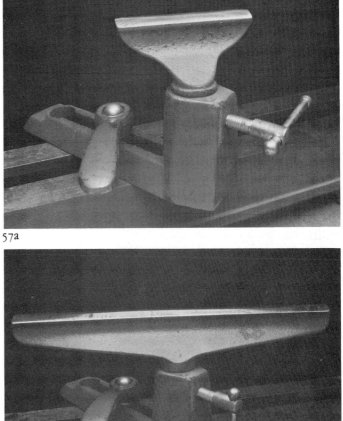

57a

57b

57c

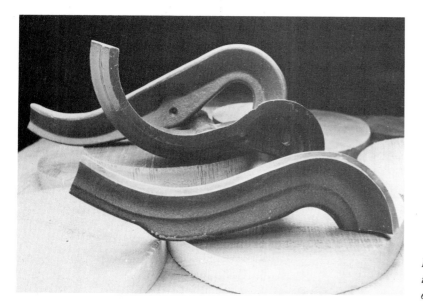

Illus. 58. Bowl-turning tool rests are usually shaped to fit the inside and outside of bowls and plates.

oted in the tool-rest base (Illus. 57a,b) to get as close as possible to the wood for maximum support and safety. The top surface of the tool rest must be smooth and straight so the tool blade can glide along it uninterruptedly. Use a bench stone to straighten and smooth this surface and follow by polishing whenever it is necessary. The tool-rest base slides along the bed of the lathe and can be tightened in any position on it.

The lathe motor (Illus. 59) provides the power that turns the headstock spindle. Lathe motors are usually positioned on the lathe in one of three ways: on the shelf of the lathe stand, directly below on the underside of the lathe table that supports the bed, or on the support directly behind the headstock. The switch for turning on the motor is usually located on the front of the stand within easy reach. A more complete discussion of motors and switches appears on pages 58–60.

Choosing a lathe. The first question that I'm often asked is "What makes a good lathe?" The answer to this question is simple. First, a good lathe is heavy. Heavy castings absorb the vibrations while turning and give the turner more control. If your lathe is light, made of light-gauge sheet metal, or has many plastic parts, you will be limited to relatively small spindles, bowls, and containers. Second,

Illus. 59. Lathe motor and switch assembly.

a good lathe should have well-machined surfaces on the tool rest and lathe bed for tools, tool-rest base, and tailstock to ride on. A well-machined surface will probably be accurate too and consistent at any setting of the tool rest or tailstock. Third, the handles and levers for adjusting tool-rest base, tool rest, and tailstock should be convenient and easy to use. Small thumbscrews or knobs are painful to work with, whereas long handles on levers or wrenches are best because they allow more leverage to tighten fixtures without exerting extreme pressure. And last, the lathe must have a threaded headstock spindle that can accept commonly available accessories. It is difficult to find chucks and faceplates for an old machine with an unusual thread. Although these cosmetic features are often the only available criteria for lathe buyers, they do provide a good starting point.

When looking at a used, older lathe follow these steps. First, look at the bearings. Any leaks around the headstock will be a clue to cracks in the bearing seals. Grab onto the spindle and give it a tug. If there is any movement in the bearings, they will have to be replaced. Second, look over all of the casting surfaces above and below. The casting should be sound and without cracks. Of course, cracks in the castings can be welded by a specialist, but that will add to the cost of the tool. The final check concerns the real accuracy of the lathe bed. Pull the tailstock over to the headstock and place the spindle centers together. If the points of the inserted centers touch perfectly when the tailstock is tightened, the tool is accurately aligned. If they do not, check to see if the tailstock fits snugly in the slot on the lathe bed. If it does not, you may be able to make it true again by replacing or modifying the worn part with an accurately sized one.

Lathe motors. The ideal motor size for lathe work is a one-horsepower (h.p.), 1725-revolutions-per-minute (r.p.m.) motor, which will provide all the power necessary for any type and size of turning. It will also run cooler under the continual load of hand turning. For smaller lathes or lathes that will be used only occasionally, a ½- or ¾-h.p. motor is satisfactory. A fan-cooled motor is typical for woodworking machines, but a totally enclosed or explosion-proof motor is not necessary.

Most new motors are sold without switches. This gives you the opportunity to custom tailor a system that is most comfortable for you. Most large motor distributors make available a broad range of switches. There are three types of switches most commonly used by turners: the toggle switch, the magnetic push-button switch, and the drum reversing switch. The toggle switch is a satisfactory system and the easiest to wire. Directions for this kind of wiring appear on the motor specification plate. The push-button magnetic switch is a little trickier to wire and can be difficult to operate if it is allowed to clog up with sawdust. The drum reversing switch (Illus. 60) is my favorite and easily the most difficult of the group to wire. Hiring an electrician to solve the puzzle will often be worth the fee. With the drum reversing switch you can reverse the rotation of the motor and consequently the rotation of the workpiece by a simple movement of the lever. This is a real time-saver when sanding end-grain patches on a plate or a bowl. This operation is explained more fully in the section on sanding (pages 202–11).

Most motors recommended for lathes revolve at 1725 r.p.m. To determine the actual speed of the turning wood use the simple

Illus. 60. The drum reversing switch facilitates reversing the rotation of the lathe motor.

equation below. It is applicable to any type or size of pulley system and is ideal for setting up a lathe to do specific types of turnings. The equation is:

$$\frac{\text{diameter of the motor pulley} \times \text{motor r.p.m.}}{\text{diameter of the headstock pulley}} = \text{headstock r.p.m.}$$

For example, a 1725-r.p.m. motor with a 3-in. (76-mm)-diameter pulley equals 5175 r.p.m. Divide 5175 by 2 for a 2-in. (51-mm)-diameter headstock pulley, and the speed at the headstock will be 2587 r.p.m., a good speed for turning a 2-in. (51-mm) spindle. By manipulating these diameters at both the motor and the headstock you can assemble an appropriate range of headstock speeds. (See also Illus. 61.)

The relevance of these speeds to the type of turning will be obvious later on, but in general slower speeds are used for turning larger, heavier wood and for sanding; faster speeds are used for turning smaller spindles under 2 in. (51 mm) in diameter and for thin plates.

Industrial heavy-duty lathes and the Shopsmith lathe feature vari-

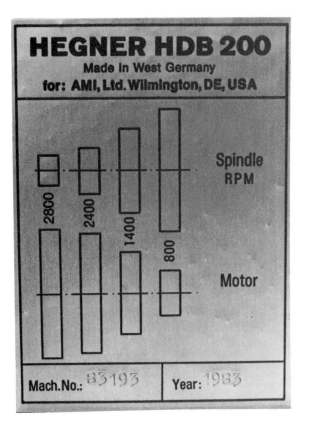

HEGNER HDB 200
Made in West Germany
for: AMI, Ltd. Wilmington, DE, USA

Spindle
RPM

2800 2400 1400 800

Motor

Mach. No.: 83193 Year: 1983

*Illus. 61. Hegner lathe pulley-speed
plate.*

able speed pulleys. By turning a dial, the diameter of the heavy-duty
pulley is changed, causing a change in the speed. This feature is
helpful because the exact speed, not just an approximate one, can be
dialled.

One point to remember when buying pulleys is that the V-groove
is sized to match a specific belt width. Belts are available in auto
parts stores in a broad range of sizes and graduated in half-inch
increments.

Lathe stand. Heavy-duty lathes are sold with heavy enclosed stands
(Illus. 62) to support the weight of the lathes and house the belt-
and-pulley system. Such stands are fabricated out of heavy-gauge,
bent sheet metal and welded at the seams. This stand is best for
heavy work, and it forms a solid unit that greatly reduces annoying
vibration when the lathe is bolted on it. Older light-duty lathes
often have heavy cast-iron stands better suited to vibration reduction
than lighter sheet-metal styles. Today, stands for light-duty lathes are
offered as options. They are sheet metal of varying thicknesses and

Illus. 62. Lathe stand. A typical design includes heavy sheet metal and welding at the seams, a heavy wooden plank on the top which adds height and absorbs vibrations, and a box filled with tools on the lower shelf, which adds even more weight.

offer only marginal additional weight and durability for their extra cost.

A good heavy hardwood, such as maple or oak, is best for building custom-made stands. They should be built to mimic the design of the old-fashioned cast-iron lathe bases. The important criteria for a good stand are splayed legs for firm support and a narrow stand top. It is tempting to actually set the lathe on a much wider top and use the remaining space to store tools while turning. I recommend that you resist this temptation and hold tools and chucks in a separate storage system. Reaching over a spindle to change tools is dangerous while the wood is turning. Tools stored on the stand top quickly get covered with dust and shavings, and fragile, sharpened edges can get nicked and damaged by striking other metal tools.

On my metal stand I place a 2-in. (51-mm)-thick maple plank between the lathe and the top of the stand. Wood absorbs a great deal of vibration, and it also helps to raise the lathe to a comfortable working height. The old maxim for arriving at the proper working height states that the height of the headstock spindle be level with

the turner's elbow. If your body is well-proportioned, this will probably work. For those with long legs or a long torso, however, this will
be too low for comfortable work. It is a good idea to use the maxim
as a starting point and then adjust the height until it is comfortable.
Only an inch or two (25 or 51 mm) will have to be added in most
cases.

The final part of the stand is the shelf, which is located about two
thirds of the way down from the top. The shelf is the usual resting
place for the motor and the most likely place to set a box of cement
blocks to increase the weight of the lathe. The shelf joins together
both sets of legs and forms a stiff rectangle with the legs and the top.
Resist storing tools and chucks on this shelf unless you plan to make
a fitted receptacle to hold them. Vibration makes them dance noisily
and fall off.

The most practical mounting for the motor base can be made simply by placing on the stand shelf two hinged pieces of wood larger
than the slotted metal base of the motor. The motor pulley should
line up with the headstock pulley exactly. The belt is kept taut by
tightening the threaded rod and wing-nut assembly that joins the
hinged wooden base together. To change speeds simply loosen this
wing nut and move the belt to the next step before tightening it up
again.

Turning-Tool Storage

Proper storage of turning tools and accessories ensures that edges
will stay sharp and that tools will be easy to reach while turning.
Good accessible storage is also unobtrusive, taking up as little floor
space as possible. If tools are kept on top of the lathe, they will soon
become dulled by contact with the cast-iron lathe and can easily slide
off onto the floor or an unsuspecting foot.

My preferred storage method is the turner's tool chest (Illus. 63).
In many ways this chest is truly derivative of the chest owned by
Rondeau (see pages 32 and 34) and used by turners for generations.
I designed this chest with a large tool capacity because of my natural
inclination to acquire more and more tools. It is long enough to
hold any of the tools that I use and has a sliding tray to hold chucks
and other smaller accessories. Calipers and other measuring devices
are stored on the inside of the lid. This keeps them from knocking
around with the other tools and becoming inaccurate. A sliding

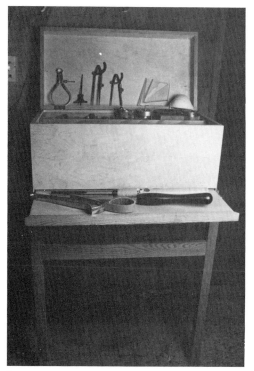

63a

63b

Illus. 63. Woodturner's tool chest. (a) This freestanding design includes a shelf for holding tools for a particular project. (b) The inside of the chest has a shelf for holding chucks and smaller tools and also a large open area for cutting and scraping tools.

shelf directly under the box pulls out to hold the handful of tools I need for each project. A raised edge on the shelf keeps the round-handled tools from rolling off. The entire chest and shelf assembly is supported on a strong mortice-and-tenon oak stand.

To keep the blades separated in the chest I use 3-in. (76-mm) lengths of shipping tubes glued together side to side in a bundle. The blades fit snugly into this arrangement and are easy to find. The plans for this storage system are shown in Illus. 64 and can be followed exactly or used as a starting point in designing your own system.

Sharpening Systems

My early experiences with sharpening devices involved a high-speed machinist's grinder and a mysterious assortment of natural and artificial hand stones. Devising fixtures for holding these tools at the right angles was simply beyond me, and in fact most of the shapes had to be ground freehand. A nicely tempered hand tool in the hands of a novice on a high-speed grinder can also lead to ruination by overheating and drawing the temper of the tool. One of the

Woodturner's Tool Chest

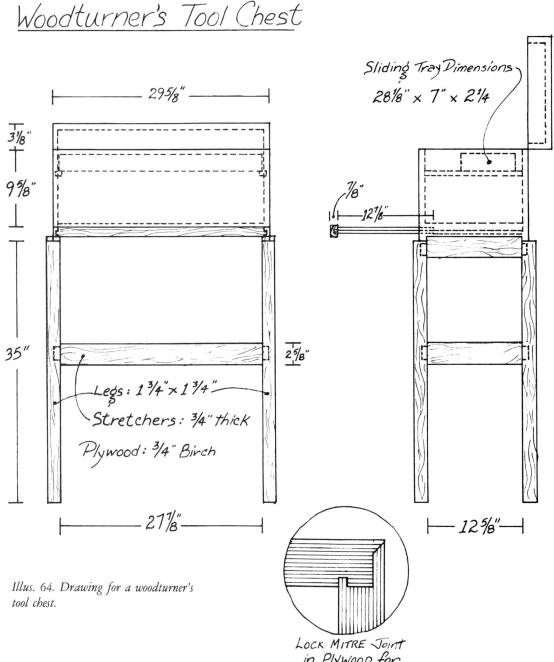

Illus. 64. Drawing for a woodturner's tool chest.

Sliding Tray Dimensions
28⅛" × 7" × 2¼

Legs: 1¾" × 1¾"

Stretchers: ¾" thick

Plywood: ¾" Birch

LOCK MITRE JOINT
in PLYWOOD for
Chest Corners

solutions that I tried was sharpening on the flat side of the grinding wheel. This is a very dangerous practice because as the abrasive is worn away on the side of the wheel it becomes weaker and can explode.

The most worthwhile approach I have found for grinding turning gouges, chisels, and scrapers is a belt grinder (Illus. 65). The system can be as simple as a belt sander turned upside down and held in a vise or as elaborate as the more expensive belt system that I use, which has a large contact wheel and an adjustable tool rest. All systems have an abrasive belt moving away from the tool, which carries away the metal filings and sparks and dissipates the heat generated while grinding. The actual grinding of the different shapes is explained on pages 78–85). After the shape has been ground, I use a buffing wheel to remove the fragile wire edge produced during the grinding process and to polish the sharpened bevel. The buffing wheel can be made of medium or firm felt or stitched muslin plies. An abrasive such as Grey's compound (aluminum oxide) is applied to the spinning wheel and the tool rubbed against it for polishing or honing. Buffing wheels can be held on a polishing head, on the arbor of a ⅓- or ½-h.p. motor, or on an accessory arbor that can be threaded onto the headstock spindle. Appropriate bench and slip-stones for sharpening individual tools are discussed on pages 78–85.

Illus. 65. Mark II sharpening system.

Workbench

There is no special bench designed for use by woodturners. The basic cabinetmaker's bench with a good sturdy vise will do the job. Woodturners often find themselves marking out blocks and hammering centers on the stand that holds the lathe or on the lathe bed itself. Unfortunately, hammering on the lathe casting can crack it. One solution is to extend the wooden board that separates the lathe from the stand over the tailstock end. This surface can then be used as an anvil for hammering or as a support for screwing on faceplates.

Band Saw

The size of a band saw (Illus. 66) is determined by the diameter of the wheels around which the saw blade travels. This is not always the critical dimension however, and it is better to know the maximum thickness of stock that can be cut on the saw and the size of the saw motor. The minimum requirements for a turner's band saw are a 6-in. (15.2-cm) cutting capacity and a ¾-h.p. motor. Coarse cutting 4- or 6-teeth-per-inch (t.p.i.) blades in ¼- or ½-in. (6- to 13-mm) sizes will handle most curves and rip spindle stock quickly from a plank. If spindle blanks must be cut with reasonable accuracy

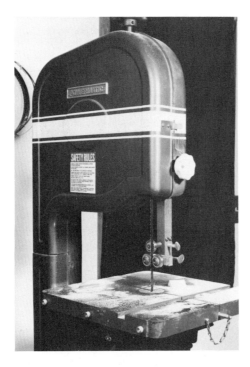

Illus. 66. Band saw. The minimum requirements for a turner's band saw are a 6-in. (15.2-cm) cutting capacity and a ¾-h.p. motor.

before planing, then use a ½- or ¾-in. (13- or 19-mm), 10 t.p.i. blade.

Safety

Safety in the shop is often neglected by well-intentioned people who don't really know what to expect of themselves and of the machines they use. Personal safety is part of good, sound work habits and will come naturally after a while if made part of the work routine. The dangers exist for all of us. A professional's odds are much better when put in the context of the thousands of hours worked. By following the techniques explained in this book and using razor-sharp tools, safe work habits will be easy to cultivate. There are a few general points, however, that should be kept in mind.

Personal safety. The part of the body that needs the most diligent protection is the face. Early in my turning career I pressed too hard on a block of wood I had screwed onto a faceplate, and an instant later I felt it bounce off my nose. Luckily I was wearing a hard rubber respirator, and the block was deflected.

Nonprescription safety glasses can cause eye strain, and tight-fitting goggles fog up from the heat. Besides the eye strain and the fogging, neither would have protected me from that flying block. Wood is not the only danger, either. Hot metal filings abraded while grinding have a way of bouncing off surfaces and heading straight for the eye. Today I use a face shield (Illus. 67). It completely covers my face down to my neck. It is clear when new and should be replaced as soon as it becomes scratched and dirty.

The second important area to protect is the lungs. Sanding dust is an irritant, and some woods are fatal to those who are particularly sensitive to them. Cocobolo is an example of a wood that produces toxic dust. Rubber respirators (Illus. 68) provide good protection against the dust entering the lungs. Those with replaceable pads are best. Many are suited for very fine particulates and can be used when spraying finishes. A paper respirator is somewhat effective against the fine sanding dust that is likely to be raised. An improvement on this simple mask is one made of fibre that fits completely over the nose and chin. But whichever style you eventually choose, it must fit snugly, especially for those with moustaches or beards. Buy the inexpensive fibre masks in bulk and use a new one each time. If planning to do a lot of turning, consider buying a vacuum system. A powerful cyclone-type separator system, which separates the air from the dust and chips, will catch most of the waste.

The remaining safety precaution is never wear loose clothing in the shop; it has a propensity to catch between the tool rest and the spinning wood.

The few accidents that I have had all occurred when working too late or too early. Don't work when you are tired; the risks far outweigh any advantages.

Machine safety. Keep wires out of the way and use heavy-wire extension cords large enough to handle the amp. rating of the motor and anything else that will be plugged into it. Pulleys and belts must be kept adequately guarded, and motors should be unplugged when changing speeds or doing other work on machines. It's also a good idea to unplug machines when not in use to protect inquisitive children.

Illus. 67. Goggles and face shield. A pair of goggles or a face shield will protect the eyes from flying chips and grinding sparks.

Illus. 68. Respirators for sanding. Left, rubber respirator with replaceable pad; right, fibre respirator.

68

67

For extra protection, lathe manufacturers have developed guards that fit over either the entire lathe bed or part of it. They were developed primarily for schools and are often required by them.

In the end, safety is simple common sense. Eliminate all the possible risks, keep an unobstructed work space, use sharp tools, and develop good work habits.

Illus. 69. The final step in rounding over a burr. See Illus. 84 for complete sequence for forming a burr on the scraper.

III · Toolmaking and Sharpening

W hat makes a good tool and how is it identified? In simple terms, a woodturning tool consists of a handle and a blade of specific size and shape designed to produce a specific cut. Several exacting factors compose a good tool.

Turning Toolmaking

Blade making. The ideal blade would be one that could slice through wood with a minimum of resistance and stay sharp for an incredible amount of time regardless of the type of wood being cut. The blades used today for woodturning are fairly primitive by modern technological standards. The methods for forging and eventual grinding of such blades are economical, simple, and hundreds of years old. The toolmaking process involves hammering a blank of steel by hand or power hammer into a die with a mating shape, trimming off the excess, and grinding the tool to a more exact shape either by hand or by machine (Illus. 70). The hardening of the tool, or the process of rearranging the molecular structure of the steel to help it reach its potential for proper edge-holding capabilities, again can be done either by machine or by hand.

There are both romantic and practical rationales for all of these methods but the ultimate tool is achieved through an approach that combines several methods. Both ancient and modern methods have their good and bad aspects. For example, tools today are mass-produced by power hammers, which force the metal into its shape, while ancient labor-intensive methods kneaded it into a tougher grain structure. Thus, failures in the less resilient mass-produced steel tools commonly appear as cracks. On the other hand, toolmakers still use a medieval method of grinding the final shape and finish of the blade. The method involves hand grinding by applying the blade to a revolving belt while straddling the wheel around which the belt revolves. Occasionally, fine work is produced, but particularly erratic results are common when toolmakers are fatigued. Certainly, modern technology could produce far more consistent results.

70b

70a

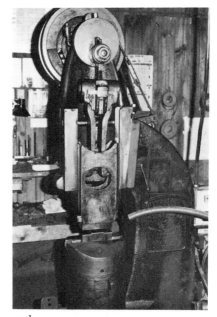

70c   70d

Blade material. Until recently, high-carbon steel was used exclusively for tools. It contains 0.03% of carbon in its structure, and this part of the formula contributes in large part to the eventual edge-holding capabilities of the tool. Carbon steel has and will continue to be an excellent material for the making of cabinetmaker's chisels and gouges, but it was never appropriate for the tools of the amateur or professional turner. It doesn't work because it is extremely vulnerable to heat. High temperatures are generated by the friction of rubbing the bevel against the revolving wood, and this friction can ruin a tool. It draws out the hardness achieved during the hardening process and actually anneals the tool. High-carbon steel is also vul-

Illus. 70. Some elements of the toolmaking process. (a) The raw material for forging tool blades can be either square, round, hexagonal, or rectangular strip steel. The heated steel can be placed on either (b) the forms of a swage block or (c) the forms of a die and hammered into shape by hand or (d) power hammer.

nerable to the friction produced by rubbing the blade bevel against a grinding belt or wheel. When the tool begins to discolor, to turn blue or black, the temper is being drawn. One alternative is to grind back to behind the discolored part, while continually quenching or cooling the tool in a water bath. The other method is to retemper the tool. Retempering the tool at home is mostly guesswork because some crucial facts about the steel are usually unknown: the critical temperature, the medium for quenching, and the gate time of the steel.

A simple explanation of the tempering process will illustrate their importance. Before a strip of steel is delivered to the toolmaker it is placed in a specific category by the manufacturer. For example, M2 has a recommended quenching medium of oil and a critical temperature of 1425 °F to 1475 °F (774 °C to 802 °C). This means that to harden this particular piece of M2 steel it must be heated to between 1425 °F and 1475 °F (774 °C to 802 °C), preferably in the 1450 °F to 1460 °F (788 °C to 793 °C) range, and then dropped into a well of oil to cool. After the steel reaches its hardening temperature, it should be released into the cooling medium within a second or two. The time that it takes to get the tool to the quench, called gate time, is very specific because hardening will not occur unless the steel cools in a precisely timed sequence. In factories, this is done automatically, and the tools are released from an electrostatically controlled heating grip into a bath below. At home, the gate time will have to be approximated, and if the tool doesn't make it in time, then the heating process will have to be repeated until hardness is achieved.

Earlier I said that carbon steel is inappropriate for turning tools. The machine industry abandoned carbon steel the day high-speed steel (HSS) was created. If you have worked with both carbon-steel and HSS router bits you are aware of the latter's superior edge-holding capability. High-speed steel is highly resistant to heat, and it is very difficult to draw its temper. The steel is relatively inexpensive, costing only four to six dollars per pound, but it does cost more to machine than does carbon steel. A well-machined tool of HSS with a smooth finish will require grinding by more and finer cutters and in addition will require some annealing operations. But such a tool, made from a good grade of HSS, will be highly resistant to heat while turning or grinding and will also be resistant to minerals and other foreign materials often found in wood. The net result of this resistance is that the tool will stay sharp 20 times longer than one made of carbon steel, which means less downtime for the professional and amateur turner.

Blade shapes. In general the tool should be bilaterally symmetrical when sighted from the cutting end of the tool. The curves should be even and smoothly ground. The blade should also be straight without any bends and anchored straight into the handle. It should be well ground, or it will be difficult to sharpen and to use. The finish should be smooth, or it will catch on the tool-rest casting. Sharpening and tuning a new blade before use is discussed in detail on pages 78–85.

Handles. Buying blades with attached handles is in some ways like hauling coals to Newcastle. It is practical, however, because such handles (Illus. 71) are usually quite acceptable and cost only pennies when made on an automatic machine. In general, the handle should fit the size and mass of the blade that it is holding. Any variation to accommodate a special purpose or style is a matter of personal preference, and the blade can usually be knocked out of the supplied handle quickly.

Tool-buying Tips

Some general guidelines should be followed when looking at tools, new or used. As a first step in checking a gouge, look down the bar-

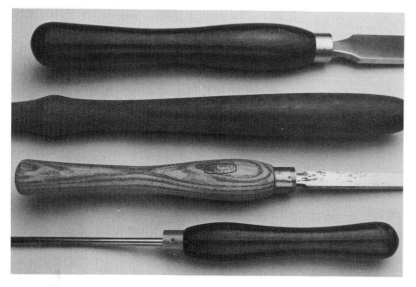

Illus. 71. Manufacturer's handles correspond to the size and mass of the blade and are usually unadorned.

rel of the blade. The shape of the blade should present a smooth even sweep with similar shapes on each side of the center line of the blade. If it is not symmetrical, it will be difficult to sharpen and unpredictable to use. Scrapers and chisels should be true rectangles, not parallelograms or some other unusual configuration. Many of these tools have been ground by hand so anything is possible. In double-bevel chisels, it is nice to have the cutting edge in the middle of the steel blank but it is not critical. You can easily regrind that part later. The last point to check while inspecting a tool is the straightness of the blade. A blade that has a crook in the middle is a plain nuisance. After ensuring that the shape of the blade is satisfactory from the barrel of the blade, look at it from the side. A little waviness along the underside of the blade is acceptable, but a bend or other exaggerated shape on this surface will lead to unpredictable turning results.

When checking the barrel of the blade for straightness, also check how the blade is seated in the handle (Illus. 72). Most turning tools have rectangular tails called tangs on the handle end, which fit into round holes. A sloppy fit is always possible. This is really a minor problem and can be fixed by knocking out the handle and hammering it back on in a different position.

Most turning tool manufacturers have standardized the simple un-

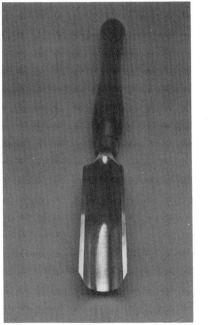

Illus. 72. (a) *Well-aligned handle on the roughing gouge.* (b) *Poorly aligned handle on the roughing gouge.*

72a   72b

adorned tool handle. The smallest embellishment added to a handle is a future blister maker, so be sure handles are simple (Illus. 73). The handle is the least critical component of the tool, since what you are really buying is the toolmaker's knowledge and ability in making the blade. Many toolmakers don't even make their own handles.

All tools require some sharpening when new. The expense of sharpening for the manufacturer is prohibitive, and most professional turners would still need to regrind the tool to their own needs. So don't let the shape of the bevel be a factor. After years of inspecting blades produced in every corner of the world, I don't even consider the condition of the bevel.

One last general rule is if the blade is coarsely ground with deep grooves, if the blade is misshapen, or if the tool in any way looks cosmetically inferior, don't buy it. It is possible to find a gem of a blade with worthwhile steel in some of these tools, but I have found that a poorly treated grinding and finishing process is usually carried out on an inferior steel or at best one of inconsistent quality.

Sharpening Turning Tools

There are so many types of sharpening systems available today that it seems impossible to teach *the* method. But some basic considerations apply to wheels, belts, and vertical or horizontal sharpening systems. As a rule-of-thumb, it is always easier to use a tool if the bevel is as flat as possible. Most circular sharpening systems leave a hollow in the center of the bevel that extends to the edge and the heel. This is a good starting point, but there must be a flat at the heel and the edge to contact the wood properly; otherwise, the tool will dig into the wood and be difficult to control. Likewise, it is difficult to control the depth of the cut with a bevel that is rounded and needs to be reground. Flat surfaces can be achieved with a hand stone of the fine India or soft Arkansas variety after the bevel has been ground. Sharpening methods differ according to tool style. The following sections detail methods for sharpening each category of turning tool.

Roughing and bowl gouges. These gouges need a cutting edge that is straight and perpendicular to the blade (Illus. 74). To achieve this shape it is important to hold the tool in the same position while grinding and to roll the edge against the abrasive (Illus. 75). This

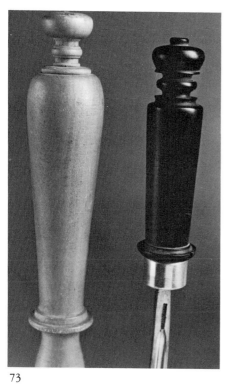

73

Illus. 73. Handmade boxwood and ebony handles with broad surfaces.

Illus. 74. These well-ground roughing gouges have cutting edges that are straight and perpendicular to the blade.

Illus. 75. Whether sharpening on a belt grinder or a grinding wheel, you must maintain the same position of the bevel in relation to the abrasive while rolling the edge.

74

75a

75b

75c

motion will ensure that all of the bevel receives equal amounts of grinding and maintains its square shape. The grinding process is finished when sparks begin to reach the edge. This may not happen equally along the entire edge, and you may have to grind a bit more in certain sections. Be careful. While the edge does not have to be perfect, it is easy to grind through and create a wavy and easily broken edge. After the entire edge is ground (Illus. 76), buff it on a muslin or felt buffing wheel coated with Grey's compound (Illus. 77). This compound is an aluminum oxide bar with the abrasive suspended in tallow or some other medium. The grade for this type of bar is usually 220 grit. Be careful not to bury the tool in the wheel or it will round over the edge.

Spindle gouges. A properly ground spindle gouge is shaped like a ladyfinger—the center of the blade at the end protrudes farther than the sides. It is important to maintain this shape for safe working, a precaution that is discussed on page 107. A new tool may not have this shape and will probably have to be reground. The sharpening method is basically the same as for the roughing gouge. By rolling the tool on the same axis in relation to the sharpening device used, the corners will be ground back and the rounded shape will appear (Illus. 78). A common problem that should be avoided in sharpening such gouges is grinding in flat sides on the cutting edge. It is often caused by placing too much pressure on the sides of the tool or spending too much time grinding each of the sides. Buff the tool (Illus. 79) after the finger shape is reached to remove the wire edge, taking care not to round over the edge.

Illus. 76. (a) The cutting edge and bevel of a newly purchased gouge is coarsely ground and nicked. After it has been ground on an abrasive belt, (b) a wire edge is formed and must be removed by buffing. (c) This is how the gouge edge looks after polishing on a buffing wheel.

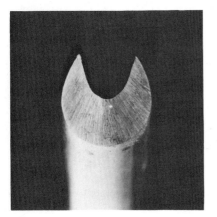

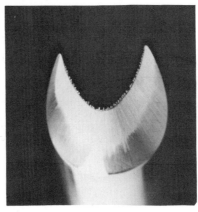

76a

76b

76c

Illus. 77. (a) *Grey's compound is positioned for application to the spinning buffing wheel.* (b) *This detail shows the Grey's compound caked onto the surface of the buffing wheel.* (c) *A rake is positioned to break the glazed surface so the plies beneath can be freed to absorb more of the compound.*

77a

77b

77c

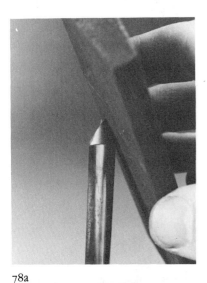

78a   78b

79

Chisels. Chisels are double-bevelled tools, and besides needing bevels that are flat, they also need sharp and well-pointed corners. On hollow-ground tools (Illus. 80) it is necessary to grind the two flat surfaces, one at the heel and the other at the cutting edge, on a stone such as a soft Arkansas or medium India. A large bench stone is best, and the sharpening procedure is the same as for any other cabinet-maker's chisel. The bevel is held down firmly against the stone (Illus. 81) and rubbed in a to-and-fro manner covering as much of the stone as possible to wear it evenly. The critical area to watch either while grinding or sharpening with a stone is the edge that is placed in the center of the tool. The final buffing can be done on the buffing wheels. A razor-sharp edge is what you are after (Illus. 82), so take time in the beginning, and it will need only an occasional buffing on the wheel while in use.

Illus. 80. (a) *Freehand sharpening of chisel edge on wheel follows the existing ground bevel.* (b) *To remove the wire edge of a freshly sharpened chisel, buff it on a wheel coated with aluminum oxide compound. Be careful not to round over the edge by pressing too hard into the buffing wheel.*

Illus. 81. *To sharpen a chisel on a hard Arkansas stone, hold the bevel down firmly against the stone and rub in a to-and-fro manner, covering as much of the stone as possible so it gets worn evenly.*

Illus. 82. *Razor-sharp edge of a chisel after it was sharpened on the stone. Flat surfaces are apparent near the edge and heel of the bevel.*

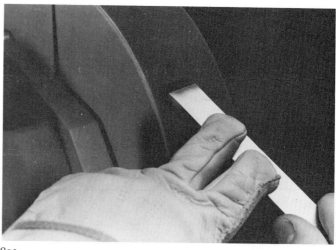

80a

80b

81

82

Scrapers. A scraper is a cutting tool like a gouge or chisel; it cuts by means of a small burr formed by burnishing or grinding and removes small shavings from the wood while cutting. Although it cannot leave a surface as smooth as a gouge or chisel, it still must remove shavings, not powder, to work properly. The simplest way to sharpen the scraper is to simply grind the entire bevel and use the wire edge that is formed as the cutting edge (Illus. 83). This works pretty well on HSS tools, but not as well on high-carbon steel tools. For carbon-steel tools, it is worth the extra effort to burnish the edge (Illus. 84) the same way in which you would a cabinet scraper. First, polish the top surface of the blade to remove any old edge. Next, grind the bevel with a fine-grit wheel or belt, or hone the bevel with a fine stone. Be sure to remove any wire edge that forms. After the top surface and bevel are smooth, take a hardened steel burnisher, either a round polished or triangular type or even the back of a chisel if nothing else is available, and draw the burnisher along the top of the blade. You must apply a little pressure here because what you are doing is pushing the steel out from the blade. This can be done with the tools lying flat on a bench top. After it is accomplished, place the blade vertically in a bench vise with the edge at the top and draw or slide the burnisher along the entire length of the drawn-out edge until it is pushed back to the top of the blade. This will be the edge that does the cutting.

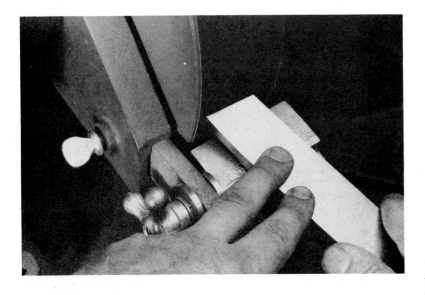

Illus. 83. Grinding the bevel of a scraper on a wheel to form a cutting edge.

84a

84b

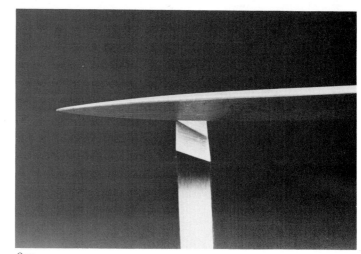

Illus. 84. Using the triangular burnisher to form a burr on the scraper:
(a) *drawing out the burr on the edge;*
(b) *first step in rounding over burr;*
(c) *final step in rounding over burr.*

84c

Illus. 85. Cutting out the spindle shape.
See also Illus. 91–96.

Illus. 86. Cutting out the vessel shape.
See also Illus. 102–105.

IV · An Illustrated Guide to the Woodturning Process

86

85

*I*t might be useful at this point to outline briefly the various woodturning processes. Full explanations for each are given later in this chapter. Methods for handling and seasoning wood used for turning have been treated out of sequence in a separate chapter, page 229, because the techniques for turning and associated concerns have been given priority in the text.

Spindle Turning

Cutting the wood. Wood for making spindles, such as chair legs, is cut to dimensions that are slightly oversized (Illus. 87) if the entire leg is to be turned completely to a round shape. If part of the leg is to have a square section or sections on it, then the spindle blank must be accurately sized and planed smooth before being marked out and mounted on the lathe.

Marking the ends. In order to locate the spindle accurately on the lathe the exact center of each end must be found. Use either a manufactured or homemade center finder (Illus. 88) to do this. It is especially important for the center points to be accurate if the leg is to contain square sections, because mismarking at this point will lead to asymmetry at the point where the turning changes from square to round. In very hard wood such as rock maple or oak, it is necessary to cut diagonal lines rather than simply marking the center with a pencil so that the spurs on the drive center will have grooves into which they can engage positively and drive the wood.

Mounting the wood. After marking the ends, use an accessory called a drive center (Illus. 89) and a mallet to make a positive impression on the ends of the wood. Place the drive center into the headstock and loosen the tailstock so that it moves freely. Put the dead or ball-bearing center into the tailstock hollow. Mount the wood between the two centers, using the impressions made on the ends as guides, and bring the tailstock up to the end of the spindle. Tighten the tailstock down onto the bed of the lathe, turn the tailstock crank to drive the center deeper into the wood, and tighten the tailstock spindle lock lever. If the drive-center end has cut diagonals in it, be sure that the drive-center spurs are well seated in these cuts. Finally, give the spindle a tug to check that it is now tightly held between the centers.

Cutting out the shape. The wood is now ready for cutting. To provide good support for the cutting tools, place the tool rest as close to the wood as possible without touching it. It must be tightly in place on the tool-rest holder and that in turn on the lathe bed (Illus. 90). It's a good idea to rotate the spindle slowly by hand to find out if there are any obstructions before turning on the motor. Be sure that the lathe is set to the appropriate speed for the type and size of the turning and cut out the shape with gouges, chisels, and scrapers (Illus. 91–96).

Illus. 87. Cutting the wood. If an entire leg is to be turned to a rounded shape, the wood must be cut slightly oversize.

Illus. 88. Manufactured and homemade center finders.

Illus. 89. Mounting the wood. Use a drive center and a mallet to make a positive impression on the ends of the wood.

Illus. 90. To provide adequate support for the cutting tools, the wood and the tool-rest holder must be tightly in place.

87

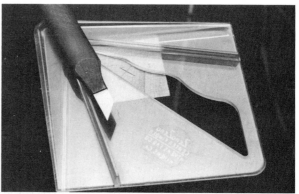

88

89

90

91

92

93

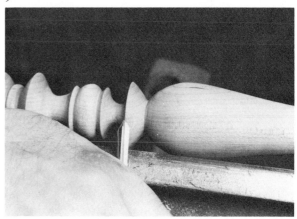

94

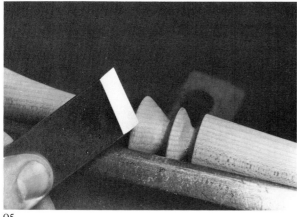

95

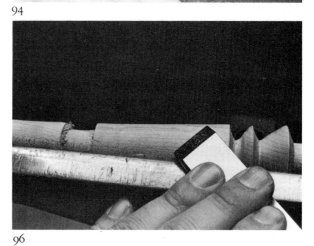

96

Illus. 91–96. Cutting out the shape. Cut out the spindle shape with gouges, chisels, and scrapers.

Sanding and finishing. After the spindle has been cut to the proper shape, if it is not highly decorated, it can be sanded with a succession of increasingly finer grades of sandpaper (Illus. 97) and steel wool and burnished with wood shavings (Illus. 98). The sanded spindle can then be removed from the lathe and stained or sealed with finishing materials.

Illus. 97. Sanding with increasingly finer grades of sandpaper.

Illus. 98. Burnishing with wood shavings.

97

98

Vessel, or Faceplate, Turning

Marking the wood. Rough measurements marked out with a pencil divider or a set of trammel points serve as an ideal guide for cutting and give a good indication of the maximum diameter possible from the board (Illus. 99).

Cutting the wood. For most one-of-a-kind bowls, plates, and containers, accurate marking is not absolutely necessary. The starting point is usually the maximum diameter or thickness that the board can yield. For round table tops and other pieces built to a plan, more careful measurements are necessary and the sawing must be done to the outside of the line, or the waste side of the line. Turning cuts can then be made up to the line for an exact dimension. For all bowls and plates, it is wise to cut out the rough shape of the blank on a band saw or with a bow saw (Illus. 100) before it is mounted on the lathe.

Mounting the block. After the block has been marked and sawed, it is ready to be mounted on the headstock of the lathe. There is a wide variety of work-holding devices (Illus. 101) designed to hold

Illus. 99. A pencil divider for marking the wood.

Illus. 100. Cutting the wood. Cut out the rough shape of the blank on a band saw or bow saw before mounting it on the lathe.

Illus. 101. Mounting the block. These work-holding devices are only a few of the many designed to secure any block of wood.

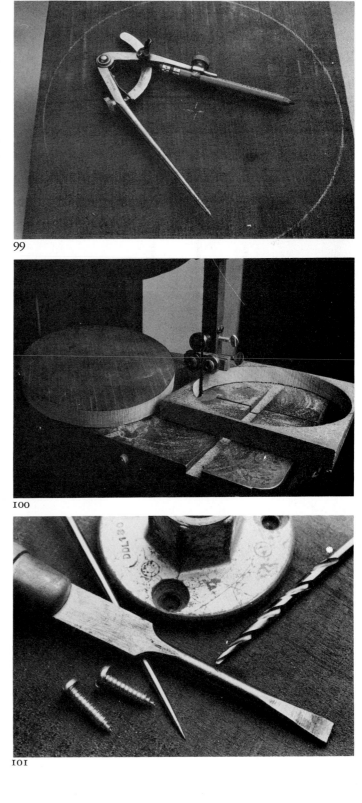

99

100

101

every conceivable block of wood, and these are explained in the vessel turning section. The appropriate methods for preparing the wood to receive these devices are also described in that chapter. Occasionally, an odd-shaped block will need additional support for the initial cutting stages, and this support can be provided by bringing up the tailstock center and tightening it against the other side of the block.

Cutting out the shape. The wood is now ready for the rough and detailing cuts that follow. Check that there are no obstructions in the way of the spinning wood by hand turning it. The speed can now be checked by quickly switching the motor on and off. Place the tool rest as close as possible to the wood to provide adequate support for the tools. The wood can be roughed out and refined with gouges and scrapers (Illus. 102–5).

Illus. 102–105. Cutting out the shape. After placing the tool rest as close as possible to the wood, rough out and refine the piece with gouges and scrapers.

102

103

104

105

Illus. 106. Sanding with increasingly finer grades of sandpaper.

Illus. 107. Burnishing with wood shavings.

Sanding and finishing. The shaped wood is sanded with a series of coarse through fine sandpapers (Illus. 106) and with steel wool, and then it is burnished with shavings (Illus. 107). The smooth piece is finally coated with stains or sealers, or both.

106

107

Illus. 108. The spindles on this Victorian porch railing were made on an automatic lathe from a hand-turned master.

V · Spindle Turning

*T*he simplest definition of a spindle is a plain or decorated, closed wooden cylinder. Because it is closed, it can be held between the centers on the lathe. The grain direction of a spindle should run from end to end and be as straight as possible, thus providing the structural integrity necessary to match its accompanying piece. Spindle turning also requires its own set of specialized turning tools, which are covered on pages 71–85.

Spindles are all around us. Besides their obvious presence in contemporary furniture and in collections of period pieces, spindles also make up a wide range of everyday items, such as knife handles and rolling pins (Illus. 109–110). Much can be learned about turned forms through the numerous examples of architectural turnings that populate houses of the Victorian era (Illus. 108). From rooftop finials to banisters and porch railings, excellent examples of manufactured and handmade spindles abound. The manufacture of turned spindles during the Victorian era required the combined efforts of the professional turner who turned the prototype, the millwright who machined the reproductions, and the knife grinder who made the cutters that were used to make the reproductions. Spindles were also produced by the patternmaker who turned spindles to exacting proportions for use as prototypes and patterns for casting moulds or

Illus. 109. Tulipwood knife handle by Ron Roszkiewicz.

Illus. 110. The parts for this modern rolling pin were machine-turned from master hand turnings.

109

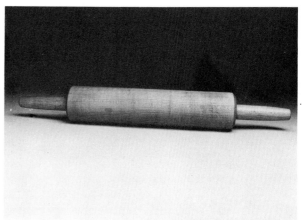

110

99

forms. Sometimes patterns were finely carved following the initial turning process. Examples of these turnings, eventually cast in metal, can be seen in iron fence posts, street-light standards, and machine tool handles (Illus. 111–113).

Technique Imperatives

While there is a lot to be said for the philosophy of doing whatever is necessary to extract a shape from the raw wood with whatever tools are either handy or can be used safely, there are certain rules of technique that must be followed to produce an elegant example of spindle turning. For example, the use of scrapers of any size or thickness on a hardwood spindle is counterproductive because such treatment produces a torn surface, which can be made acceptable only by the abrasion of successive grades of sandpapers. Sanding is antithetical to the crisp shapes and lines that constitute an elegant turning because the ideal way to sand a spindle is with the grain, and this is not possible if there is any decoration on it. Thus, scraping and sanding restrict the shapes that can be made to very simple forms that are better produced by machines.

And so the attraction for large, broad vessel shapes among modern woodturners becomes clear. It would seem better to attempt to stretch the limits and standards set by cabinetmakers and turners during the 18th century, the golden age of woodworking. A well-

Illus. 111. Cast-iron fence posts, like the one shown here, were made from a group of hand-turned patterns.

Illus. 112. This cast-iron fire hydrant was made from a group of hand-turned wooden patterns.

Illus. 113. This chromed, die-cast machined handle was made from a hand-turned wooden master.

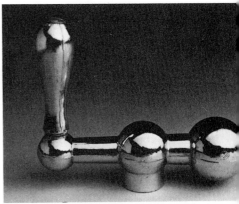

113

111

112

made spindle is cut, never scraped. The crisp cut edges and fair curves on the undercut surfaces of an elegantly cut spindle require total control of razor-sharp cutting tools and the dexterity to leave a smoothly burnished surface behind. No sanding should be necessary to obtain a surface that actually glows. Thus the spindle turning section in this book emphasizes cutting technique more than any other.

Commonsense Design

The shapes and forms, diameters and tapers that comprise a spindle may or may not work. Although design is subjective, the resolution of the work as a whole must be considered. The turned elements of a table should contribute to its most important function, while at the same time aesthetically resolve within themselves. Take for example a highly ornate, carved set of legs. If placed on a breadboard-ended trestle table, the effect would be two very different styles fighting for attention, and the piece would become a mere curiosity. But placed on a recessed, scallop-lipped, piecrust table top, those same legs—with their mass and carvings complementing the moulded edge of the top—would create a harmonious whole.

This balance is important in banisters and porch railings in which spindles are used as a group. They create texture through shadows and harmony through symmetry. Spindle placement is important, and group integrity can be compromised by careless spacing. While the symmetry of the individual spindle may resolve itself, the group as a whole must work within the limits of the banister.

The Vocabulary of Spindle Shapes

There is a basic group of shapes from which all spindle variations and sizes originate. The combinations and intermixing of shapes produce infinite patterns.

Square. The square (Illus. 114) is the initial shape in many designs. For example, in a table leg the square may be the shape that is joined to the table apron at the top of the leg. In its roughest shape, it is an unplaned, approximately square block from which a completely round decorated cylinder might be turned. But for a square-topped leg, the square wooden block must be planed smooth with all sides square to each other and the exact center at each end precisely located. Another option is to leave the approximately square end of leg rough and unturned and carve details after the other shapes on the leg have been turned.

Cylinder. The cylinder is usually the next step in the spindle turning process. A rough-turned cylinder (Illus. 115) can serve as the simple surface on which pattern measurements are transferred for future cutting, or it can be planed smooth (Illus. 116) to become a design element in itself.

Cone. The cone shape (Illus. 117) is a variation of the cylinder and is made with the same tools. It too can be a design element alone or serve as the basis for further decoration.

Cove. The cove is the broad term for all hollow shapes (Illus. 118) on the spindle regardless of length or diameter.

Bead. Beads are round, half-round, or oval shapes (Illus. 119) that can also vary in length or diameter.

Undercut shape. This shape is usually associated with the cove (Illus. 120). It is definitely an accentuation of the basic hollow shape and lends lightness and delicacy to the basic form.

Spindle-turning Tools and Drilling Tools

The tools that I feel are necessary to the practice of spindle turning are discussed in this section. They have changed little in hundreds of years, and when well made they are lean, well-balanced tools. Those

Illus. 114. Square blanks.

Illus. 115. Roughed cylinder.

114

115

116

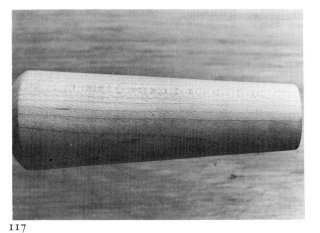

117

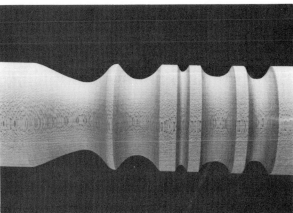

118

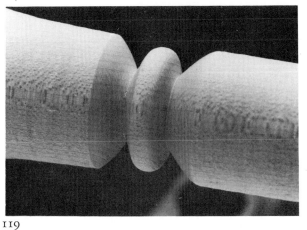

119

Illus. 116. Planed cylinder.

Illus. 117. Planed cone.

Illus. 118. Group of cove shapes.

Illus. 119. Bead shape.

Illus. 120. The undercut shape is clearly revealed on the rough side of a split turning.

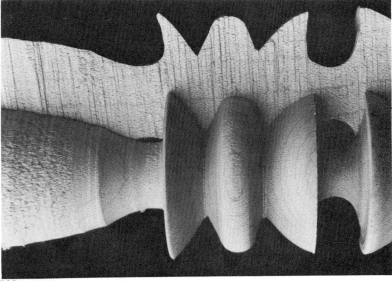

120

made in Britain and the United States differ from the ones made in continental Europe. British and American tools are virtually identical in size and shape. They are largish tools with a fair amount of meat to the blade. As a rule, continental European tools are more delicate with smaller blades and handles. Which is better? Detailing or nonroughing gouges seem to work better with smaller handles: the cut is fine, the tool rest is close, and no special handle leverage is needed. This also holds true for the ½-in. (13-mm) skew chisel. For all the others, the longer handle–longer blade combination is easier to work with. At the end of this section are recommendations for both an abridged and an expanded turning-tool set. You can't do the work without the right tools.

Roughing gouge. Each area of woodworking requires a tool for removing large amounts of wood from the surface, a preliminary tool that prepares the surface for future decoration. In most cases, the roughing gouge serves this function. This is also true in woodturning. Except when preparing small spindles, the roughing gouge is the first tool used to reduce the size and shape of a blank of wood from a square to a rough cylinder.

The cross-section view of the gouge reveals a shape like a deep "U" with high sides (Illus. 121). The side view shows that the cutting end of the tool is ground straight across and the bevel is short (Illus. 122). The reason for the U-shape and straight-across grind at the cutting end is to allow the tool to make a deep cut in the wood, removing as much material as possible in one pass and scoring the long grain of the wood. The high sides of the blade score in much

Illus. 121. The cross-section view of a roughing gouge is shaped like a deep "U" with high sides.

Illus. 122. The side view of a roughing gouge shows that the end is ground straight across and that the bevel is short.

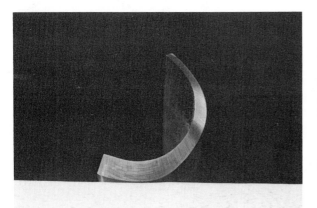

121

122

the same way as two knife blades work to eliminate tearing. A comparison between the cutting action of the shallow spindle-type gouge and the deep-cutting roughing gouge graphically illustrates the difference blade shape can make. The shallow gouge tears the wood, and if too deep a cut is attempted, it can chip out large chunks of the wood.

The most common sizes for roughing gouges are ¾, 1¼, and 1½ in. (19, 32, 38 mm). For the amateur, the ¾-in. (19-mm) gouge is perfectly satisfactory and will provide a clean cut. For the professional, however, the larger sizes are preferred because wood can be removed much faster, and time is money.

The roughing gouge is a coarse cutting tool and requires no special tuning, other than sharpening, to make it a precision instrument. The bevel of a roughing gouge is short, but it is still about twice the thickness of the steel in the center of the tool. You should try as best you can to keep the end of the tool straight across, although slight variation will not greatly affect the performance of the tool. If the gouge is sharpened on a fine grit wheel or belt (60-grit wheel, or 100-grit belt) little or no honing will be necessary. This is a rough cutting tool and will not need a fine bevel because this tool cannot be depended upon to produce the finely finished surface desired on the wood.

Parting tool. The parting tool is a coarse cutting chisel with a very narrow cutting edge perpendicular to the sides of the blade. The tool is used for making straight-in cuts to identify diameters, form tenons, and to make the deep incising cut that splits the spindle into two pieces. The techniques for the use of this tool will be explained shortly, but for now it is important to mention that the types of cuts made with this tool cause a great deal of friction. Friction of this sort can draw the temper of a carbon-steel tool and can also cause the tool to kick back dangerously. So tool users and some manufacturers have devised ways to solve both problems. The illustrations show some of their design solutions.

The first example is the simple beading and parting tool (Illus. 123). It is basically a square shank of tool with two bevels ground at the end. It doesn't really solve the friction problem as a parting tool, but it does have redeeming virtues as a beading tool, which are discussed on page 150. The fishtail parting tool (Illus. 123) has a rectangular shank with two bevels and also two ground sides that produce a bit of relief behind the cutting edge reducing metal-to-wood contact and thus friction. This approach does the job pretty well, but after only a few sharpenings the sides must be ground away to provide that relief once again. The last is the diamond style (Illus. 123), which has facets on both sides to remove as much metal-to-wood contact as possible and still provide a reasonable width at the cutting edge. The two wide ridges cause little friction, and the shape of the blade does not change as the edge is ground back.

The parting tool is called a coarse cutting tool because it does not have the high sides of a gouge that score the cross-grain fibres and make a clean cut. It tends to tear and leave a feathery edge in the end grain (Illus. 124). Manufacturers have attempted to solve this problem by grinding the underside of the blade into a long hollow channel with two high ridges along the sides. When a bevel is ground along the straight-across edge, these two ridges form ears at the cutting edge, which score the end-grain fibres and leave a smooth surface. The hollow-ground parting tool performs best by leaving the fibres smoothly cut as it enters the wood (Illus. 124). It is not the ultimate tool for shearing the fibres all along the cut, and the result-

Illus. 123. Parting tool shapes: beading, fishtail, and diamond.

Illus. 124. The hollow-ground parting tool, left, *makes a clean cut, but the diamond-shaped parting tool,* right, *makes a coarse cut.*

123

124

ing surface usually needs additional work with the skew chisel. It does stay sharp longer because of its design and may be a little quicker cutting than the more common nonhollow tool. When using such a tool, be sure to wrap cloth tape around the area where it comes in contact with the tool rest because sharp ridges tend to score the soft castings of tool rests.

The parting tool is easy to sharpen. Any type of grinding device can be used, and the edges can be honed on a stone after grinding or buffed on a buffing wheel. Because it is a coarse cutting tool, most professional turners simply use the tool directly after grinding with only a nominal amount of buffing to remove the wire edge. It is important to remember to keep the cutting edge in the center of the tool. The length of the bevel should be similar to the diamond-shaped parting tool in Illus. 124, but this is not a critical angle.

Spindle gouges. The hollow shapes that form much of the decoration on a spindle are made with spindle gouges. There is a wide range of spindle-gouge sizes, from ¼ to 2 in. (6 to 51 mm) in width, because of the different sizes of coves or hollows they must make (Illus. 125). The smallest size obviously works best on a delicate finial for, say, the top of a grandfather clock, while the largest would be just the thing for a support column on a public building. The two critical elements of the spindle gouge, regardless of its size, are the depth of the channel in the center of the tool and the shape of the nose on the end of the tool (Illus. 126). The even, rounded shape of the sides of the gouge together with the moderate depth of the center channel combine to provide proper depth of cut with a shearing action that leaves a smooth surface behind. Some of the available spindle gouges and the variations in their depths are shown in Illus. 127. Too shallow a tool will always get in the way because it is primarily thick steel and bevel rather than curved cutting edge.

The first thing to do after buying a new gouge is to resharpen the nose. The tools in Illus. 128 show the wide variation among factory-ground ends. The proper shape should be very much the same as the tapering of a finger (Illus. 129). There must be even curves on each side without facets or flats. While the rounded tip does some of the work, the sides do most of the cutting. For most spindle work on furniture parts, spindle sizes of ¼, ⅜, and ½ in. (6, 10, 13 mm) are the most useful and are worth owning.

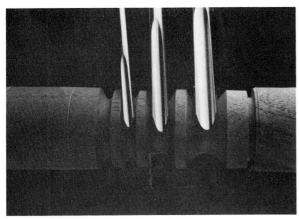

125

127

126

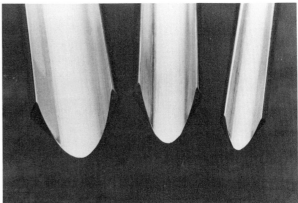

128

129

Illus. 125. Spindle gouges range in size from ¼ in. (6 mm) to 2 in. (51 mm) wide, according to the size cove or hollow they must make.

Illus. 126. The spindle gouge has sym-metrically shaped sides and is moderately deep in the center channel.

Illus. 127. The illustration shows some of the available spindle gouges and their various depths.

Illus. 128. The illustration shows the wide variation among factory-ground ends.

Illus. 129. The end of a spindle gouge is shaped like a ladyfinger.

The only bit of tuning usually needed on a new spindle gouge is polishing the inside channel of the blade near the cutting edge. This top surface determines the strength of the cutting edge. If the inside channel and the outside bevel are both polished with fine-grit abrasives, the edge will become what is called consolidated and form a strong bevel.

Skew and square-ended chisels. The chisel serves many purposes for the turner. It is in some ways like the smoothing plane that shaves a smooth top surface on a plain undecorated surface, and it is sometimes like a paring knife for peeling away layers of wood and exposing a smooth inside. Chisels are made of a blank of steel with a couple of bevels on one end. It's such a simple tool. It is available in a range of sizes, usually from ½ to 2 in. (13 to 51 mm); the former is of course for delicate turnings and the latter for massive surfaces. For spindle turning the ½-in. (13-mm) and 1¼-in. (32-mm) sizes are used most often.

One important tuning-up exercise is worth doing as soon as you get the tool. On most new tools the corners that run along the tool from end to end are sharp, just as they were left after the four surfaces of the tool were ground. These sharp corners can easily catch in a ridge or hollow on the tool rest and cause a loss of control. It's important to grind the corners off and make them round, polishing them later (Illus. 130) so that they will glide along a similarly polished tool rest. On many old turning tools, I have found, this rounding was taken to an extreme, and the corners near the cutting edge were ground away into very broad chamfers. It might be worthwhile to round over the narrow surfaces completely, which would result in even better control.

Skew and square-ended chisels must have flat bevels (Illus. 131). The most critical flat area on the bevel is near the cutting edge itself. Flattening is easily done on a bench stone, and a little polishing can be done on a buffing wheel. It is important to achieve and maintain extremely sharp and pointed corners because they pierce the wood and help establish the depth of cut. If the corners are not sharp, it will be difficult to penetrate the wood. Treat this tool like any cabinetmaker's paring chisel.

Scraping tools. The name scraping tool is in many ways misleading, but only because the tool seems to be used for a different effect than

130

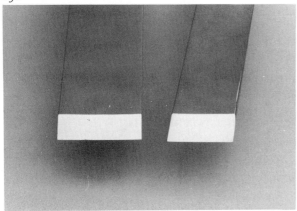

131a

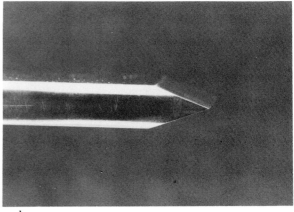

131b

a cutting tool is. Although the majority of all cutting on spindles is done with the cutting tools mentioned previously, occasionally it is feasible and appropriate to use small- to medium-sized scraping tools to make very small or extremely ornate designs. They work particularly well when used to cut exotic materials such as ebony and ivory. For most cutting on other materials, even on hardwoods, the surface left by scraping tools is too coarse and requires too much sanding. Scraping tools for work in exotic materials can be made of any available piece of steel, masonry nails, old multiplane cutters, chisels, files; any hardened piece of steel will do. They can be shaped to suit the shape of the desired cut. The very heavy scrapers are designed for vessel or faceplate turning and will be discussed later.

One bit of tuning that I like to do is to polish the top surface of the scraper (Illus. 132). The smooth top surface gives increased stability for better cutting after the bevel edge has been sharpened by burnishing or grinding. But that's all I need to do to a scraper. The

Illus. 130. Detail of a chamfer (bevelled edge) that has been ground and polished on the long edge for better control.

Illus. 131. (a) Square-ended and skew chisels; (b) side view, critical flat bevel.

bevel on scrapers is usually short if you use the simple grinding method to form a cutting edge. When burnishing the edge to form the cutter, it is best to make a longer bevel. In this way you can make a substantial burr on the end, which can be adjusted as necessary. See Illus. 133 for how the pointed end of the triangular burnisher is used to adjust the position of the burr. In either case, a finer grit-grinding abrasive will produce a stronger, longer-lasting burr, particularly on high-speed steel tools.

Drilling tools. In principle, the basic lathe can be used as a drill press. In truth, it is practical only for a few woodturning-related operations. One such operation is removing wood from the hollows of bowls and containers. The best drill for this is the multispur machine bit (Illus. 134), which has a number of sawlike teeth around the top perimeter and either one or two straight cutters with spaces in front for clearing out the waste wood. Although it is the quickest cutting of the bits available and even with its coarse-cutting configuration, it still must be pulled periodically from the hole it is making to minimize the heat caused by friction and binding. The two-cutter style runs cooler than the one-cutter. The center point on these bits must be a plain spur type. The screw center-feed type favored by electricians clogs up quickly at high speeds and at normal feed rates,

Illus. 132. Polished top surface of a scraper.

Illus. 133. The pointed end of a triangular burnisher adjusts the position of the burr.

132

133

and the resulting blunt point makes drilling difficult. Multispur machine bits leave a center-point indention and a perimeter-cutting line at the bottom of the drilled hole. For most operations this is acceptable because the drilled hole will not be the eventual finished surface depth. The finish cutting will be done with turning tools. If there is a need for a more finished hole, resort to using a Forstner bit. (This type of bit, however, does not leave a perfect bottom either, because it also has a central locator point and a cutting rim that is higher than the main cutter.) Small-hole drilling is best done with brad-point drills. The combination of a central point and one or two side spurs centers the drill and cuts true, removing wood quickly.

Drill bits should be held in a Jacob's or 3-jaw chuck, which is in turn fitted into the quill of the tailstock. There are two types of 3-jaw drill chucks (Illus. 135): the key chuck that is tightened with a geared key, and the keyless chuck that is tightened with hand pressure alone. Of the two, I have had the best luck with the key chuck. It holds the bit tight enough to withstand the constant pressure to loosen.

Long hole drilling into the end grain of a lamp standard requires a long-shanked bit such as the shell auger or the electrician's bit. The shell auger is a blunt-nosed cutting tool with a cutter and a deep, hollow, chip-collecting section behind it. The shell auger is designed to be fed into the wood by hand, and it would be impractical to try to use it in a chuck. It is a good idea to put either a T-handle or a straight handle, similar to a chisel handle, on the end. The best way to locate and guide in the auger is with a device called the hollow-boring guide. This device, rather than the tailstock, holds the end of the spindle and is secured in the tool-rest base. The guide is available in a variety of sizes to match the different bit sizes, but is not usually larger than ½ in. (13 mm) because most drilling of this type is done to accommodate the lamp wire.

On most lathes, the tailstock quill can be advanced into the wood by turning the handle in the same way as a center would be tightened into the wood. It is also possible to advance the bit into the wood with the tailstock completely loosened on the lathe bed and the entire assembly pushed into the wood.

The speeds for drilling wood should be moderate, and the rate of feed into the wood should also be moderate. Follow the speed instructions supplied by drill manufacturers and adapt speed and feed

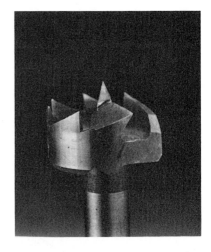

Illus. 134. The multispur machine bit is best for removing wood from the hollows of bowls and containers.

Illus. 135. Jacob's or 3-jaw chuck. The key chuck, left, is tightened with a geared key, and the keyless chuck, right, is tightened with hand pressure alone.

to suit the type of wood and the size of the bit. If the friction of the bit action in the wood causes burning, it is usually because the wood that has been cut away is clogging the hole. Simply clear out the chips more often.

Multispur and brad-point drills can be sharpened without too much difficulty. Smooth mill files or triangular-tapered India sharpening stones can be used with good results. When sharpening brad-point drills, it is important not to take away too much steel on the already delicate side-cutting spurs (Illus. 136). Never change the outside dimensions of the bit and do all filing on the inside of the spurs. The two clearing cutters just inside of the spurs should be filed on the underside. Only a little bit of metal needs to be removed to make the bit useful again. If the damage to this type of bit is too great, it would make sense to grind off the end and change it into a twist drill in a drill-grinding device.

Multispur bits can be sharpened on the top or front surfaces of the cutting teeth (Illus. 137). When sharpening this bit be sure to keep the height of the teeth the same all the way around the bit for equal cutting (Illus. 138). The single or double clearing cutter should be sharpened on the underside and every attempt must be made to keep this cutter as straight as possible. One easy way to check the height of the cutters on the perimeter is to punch a hole in a straight piece of card and place it on top of the bit to see if any daylight falls between the card and the cutter.

Illus. 136. The brad-point bit must be sharpened with care so that a minimum amount of steel is removed from the delicate side spurs.

137a

137b

137c

Illus. 137. Sharpen multispur bits on (a) the top or (b) the front surfaces of the cutting teeth. (c) Sharpen the single or double clearing cutter on the underside.

Illus. 138. The height of the cutters on multispur bits should be uniform.

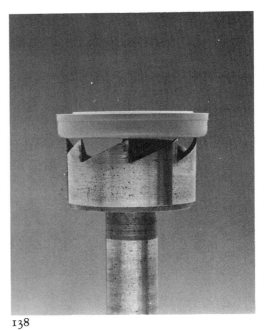

138

The Basic Tool Kit

One of the most difficult problems that beginning turners face besides lathe selection and skill building is selecting the basic tool kit. Sets packaged by tool companies today may be produced in response to current literature, to a competitor's set, or to the known popularity of the individual items. My basic starter set included the following: a parting tool, ¾-in. (19-mm) roughing-out gouge, ¼-in. (6-mm) spindle gouge, ½-in. (13-mm) spindle gouge, ½-in. (13-mm) skew chisel, 1-in. (25-mm) skew chisel, ½-in. (13-mm) roundnose scraper, and a 1-in. (25-mm) roundnose scraper. These tools will make most any cut normally encountered in spindle and bowl turning. See pages 123–53 and 184–201 for exercises using these tools. It will soon become apparent that the ½-in. (13-mm) spindle gouge and the 1-in. (25-mm) skew chisel are used the most. They should be at the top of the list when buying tools. As the range of your work expands, the need for larger and smaller scrapers, gouges, and chisels will become obvious. Wait until then to purchase additional sizes, and in the meantime work to expand the uses of those tools in the basic set.

A basic set of sharpening equipment should include a belt grinder, combination coarse and fine bench stone, soft Arkansas natural bench stone, round-edged soft Arkansas slip stone, and a muslin or felt buffing wheel with an aluminum oxide abrasive, like Grey's compound.

Marking the Spindle

The first step in preparing the spindle for mounting on the lathe is to mark the ends of the piece in order to locate the center points. This can be either a critical or noncritical operation depending on the ultimate design and use of the spindle. If for example the spindle is to be used as a table leg and the design incorporates a square section near the top that will be joined to the apron surrounding the table, the precise location of the center points on the ends will be necessary. Squaring and planing smooth the spindle blank is required beforehand because it is too difficult to do after the turning has been completed. Any inaccuracy in marking the dead centers will appear in unbalanced details at the point where the square joins the rounded section of the turning. When the entire blank of wood is to be turned round, it is critical to have only enough wood in the blank to accommodate the largest diameter on the proposed turning. The center points can be more approximate in this situation.

The precise center of a square, planed blank of wood is located with a center finder (Illus. 139). It has two blades that form a 90° angle into which the wood fits; a third blade bisects that angle and forms a 45° angle from which a diagonal can be marked to join each set of corners in turn. The most accurate way to mark a line against the bisecting blade is to use a single bevelled knife. The unbevelled side rubs flush against the bisecting blade at the center of the blank. It is safest to do this operation on each corner of the square blank in order to locate any inaccuracies that might have occurred because of imprecise planing or other machining operations. If there is an inaccuracy, indicated by a line that doesn't overlap another line, check first that the line was made properly with the knife blade flush against the center finder's blade. If this was done accurately, then the problem would be with the wood, and it should be replaned to even out the inaccuracy.

After some years of turning experience, it will be possible to eyeball the approximate center of the ends for all noncritical work. You can also use a pencil with the center finder instead of a knife. If a center finder is not available, use a ruler to find the diagonals, corner to corner. But I have never had good luck with this method because the ruler always seems to slip and the corners are not always sharp and easy to identify. Although the pencil line is thick, it is acceptable for noncritical work.

Some people recommend sawing the diagonals into the drive end, or headstock end, of the blank so that the spurs on the drive center will engage the wood better. I have never found this to be necessary if the spurs are kept sharp. For critical work this method would be impossible to control and would necessitate an inordinate amount of time to make an accurate cut.

After the centers have been found, hammer the drive center into the ends so that an impression is made (Illus. 140). The spindle end, located on the headstock end of the lathe, requires a strong impression so that the spurs will engage deeply, but the tailstock end does not require anything more than a center point. I prefer to use a lead-filled rubber mallet to supply the shock necessary to penetrate the wood without damaging the end of the drive center. Don't use the ball-bearing center to make these impressions because it could damage the bearings.

Illus. 139. Marking tools: left, clear-plastic center finder with scribing compass and single-bevelled knife; right, pencil compass and calipers.

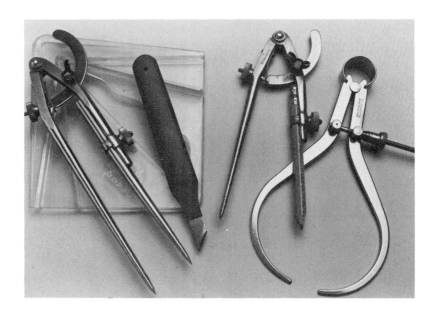

Illus. 140. Hammer the drive center into both ends of the wooden blank to ensure accurate and deep engagement in the headstock and tailstock.

Mounting Devices

Drive centers. There are a handful of different mounting centers for spindle work. The first is the drive center. This is the tool used to mark the locator points in the ends of the wood blank, and it will be the device that engages the wood and turns it with the motor on. Drive centers have a center point and two or more chisel-like spurs radiating out from the center. The center point can be either fixed or removable. The spurs must be as sharp as possible to engage the wood deeply without extreme force from the tailstock end. The bevels on the spurs must be sharpened, and this can be done with a file or by grinding against the machine grinder. Care must be taken to keep the cutting edges at the same height or as close as possible for the best grip. On some drive centers, the center point can be removed and adjusted for penetration at different depths. This is a handy feature because it is possible to resharpen it by removing the point, holding it in a pair of vise-grip pliers, and rotating it against an abrasive belt or wheel. This is a rare situation, however, and for most touching up the removable center point can be left in the center but extended out to its limit and trued using a fine piece of crocus cloth with the lathe turning, but beware of those revolving spurs and wear gloves just in case.

The three common types of drive centers are the Morse taper, the screw on, and the screw in. Identified by a Morse taper designation, the first type is available in three sizes: No. 1, No. 2, and No. 3. The dimensions for each are given in the appendix. The Morse taper (Illus. 141) is the most common of all types and is supplied with most lathes. It is held in the spindle of the headstock by a press fit.

A device called the minidrive center is an optional drive center that solves the problem of making a small tenon on the end of a spindle designed to fit into a chair seat or stetcher. The minicenter can be only ⅜ in. (10 mm) in diameter, much smaller than the ¾ or 1 in. (19 or 25 mm) of the larger centers.

Tailstock centers. Most lathes are sold with what is known in the turning trade as a dead center. It is called dead because it remains stationary in the tailstock quill and does not revolve with the work. The common practice is to lubricate it with wax or oil. If the same dead center is used on a regular basis, I suggest using a scented oil because the burning smell may be offensive. The more common practice is to buy a ball-bearing center to replace it. The ball-bearing center revolves with the work and is lubricated for life. Actually, it is lubricated for life only if you turn a few hours a week and no more. I have worn out a couple already.

The most common type of ball-bearing center is the Rockwell brand (Illus. 142). It has a set of three interchangeable heads and fits into the tailstock with a Morse tapered shank. The most used center is the cup head, which locates the center of the wood with the head point and holds the wood with the grip of the cup that surrounds it. The cup compresses the fibres against the point but it does tend to get bunged up and lose its effectiveness over time. The second type of head is the 60° point, used most often in metal turning in the United States, but commonly used for woodturning in Britain and continental Europe. It works fine for woodturning, and because of its simplicity can be trued without much difficulty. The third interchangeable head is called the pad head. This head has been most useful to me in supporting off-sized blanks of wood for bowl turning during the initial rounding process. It supposedly can be used for drilling with the drill chuck in the headstock and the pad head acting as a support for the wood being drilled, but I have never used that method. When the interchangeable head is removed from the

Illus. 141. The Morse taper is the most common drive center.

ball-bearing center a hollow remains, and it is possible to use the hollow to fit homemade plug heads and other types made of wood for special applications.

The illustration shows a selection of different types of ball-bearing centers. The Rockwell brand with interchangeable heads is common among woodturners but does not have the same lasting qualities as the machinist's single-head, 60° point center. Since the machinist's centers are usually two or three times the price of the Rockwell, the real bargains are the adaptable centers available from Sears Roebuck and Company. If the hole in the quill of the lathe is sized to fit a No. 2 Morse taper and the Sears center is a No. 1 Morse taper, buy an adapter sleeve from any machinist supplier, which changes the center taper from the smaller No. 1 to the larger No. 2.

Steady rest. The steady rest is a very important ally in turning spindles, and it's amazing how few people actually have one. They are generally thought of as supports for thin, long turnings, but in truth they can be used frequently for turnings that have only one or two slender sections. The steady rest is composed of three or more adjustable arms with ball bearings attached (Illus. 143). The arms are joined to a larger C-shaped holder that surrounds the spindle and is clamped to the bed of the lathe. The ball-bearing arms are adjusted to contact the wood, moving with the wood and supporting it while turning, because under pressure of the headstock and tailstock, the wood can whip at high speeds, particularly when lateral pressure is

Illus. 142. Rockwell ball-bearing center with three interchangeable heads.

Illus. 143. The steady rest provides additional support for long, thin spindles.

142

143

applied with the turning tool. The steady rest is moved along the lathe bed to facilitate working on any part of it. Steady rests can be homemade or purchased ready-made.

The number of other types of mounting devices could and probably will fill another book. These are the basic ones for spindle turning and should be able to handle nearly all of the usual operations.

Mounting the Blank on the Lathe

The first step in the turning process, after the wood has been marked and the centers have been located, is mounting the wood on the lathe. The center impressions on the end of the spindle (Illus. 144) destined for the headstock must be deep and positioned to match with the center point and spurs on the drive center (Illus. 145), which is already inserted in the headstock. The ball-bearing center should also be inserted in the tailstock, and the opposite end of the spindle fitted into it (Illus. 146). The next step is to tighten up the tailstock into the wood by completely loosening the tailstock quill with the tailstock itself clamped securely onto the bed of the lathe. Tighten the quill firmly without extreme pressure. Check that the tailstock is not moving along the lathe bed as you tighten, and if it is, apply more pressure to the tailstock clamp. When tightening the quill into the wood, try not to let the quill extend too far out of the tailstock as this might compromise its seat in the tailstock. By allowing an inch and a half (38 mm) or so, you can back off, remove the wood, and mount another piece of equal size after turning without moving the tailstock on the bed. With pressure applied to the wood, lock the quill-locking mechanism. The pressure applied to the wood by the tailstock compresses the fibres of the wood, and this compression tends to loosen during turning. If you hear a rattle when applying a cutting tool to the wood, check the pressure of the tailstock by loosening the quill-locking lever and turning the tailstock handle slightly to advance the ball-bearing center into the wood a bit more.

After the wood is securely mounted between centers, it is time to position the tool rest close to, but not touching, the wood. For spindle turning it is important to place the top of the tool rest below the center line formed by the two center points (Illus. 147). The exact placement is dependent upon the tool that is intended for first use and also upon the turner's height and the height of the lathe.

Illus. 144. The drive-center impressions on the wooden blank must be deep and easily matched to the drive center after it is inserted into the headstock.

145

146

Illus. 145. Wooden blank engaged into headstock drive center.

Illus. 146. Wooden blank engaged into tailstock ball-bearing center.

Illus. 147. The tool-rest position for spindle turning is below the center line formed by the two center points.

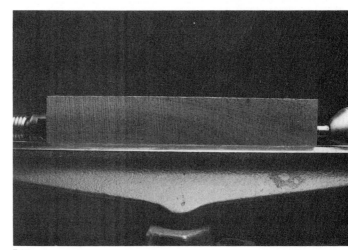

147

Tool-rest position will be covered in detail as each shaping technique is discussed, but in general the tool rest is always below center when using cutting and scraping tools. Rotate the wood fully at least once to see if the rest obstructs the free movement of the wood in any way. If it does, readjust the rest, rotate, and check once again.

The lathe is now ready to turn on, and the first decision is what speed to use for the size of the turning. Approximate speeds for different size spindles are listed in the Appendix (page 245). The working principle is to use the highest speed possible without causing too much vibration and losing control (Illus. 148). The higher the speed, the smoother the surface can be. On a variable speed lathe it is easy to dial up the speed as high as it can go and back off if the vibration gets too great. As a rule, a speed in the range of 2100 r.p.m. for all spindles 2½ in. (64 mm) and larger is appropriate. Spindles 2 in. (51 mm) and smaller can be cut best at speeds in the 2800 r.p.m. and higher range.

Safety

It's always nice to know what possible danger you might encounter in a tool. The lathe can be intimidating at first, but confidence will grow in direct proportion to your experience on the machine. Following are some safety-related matters regarding the initial mounting of the wood, positioning the rest, and turning on the machine.

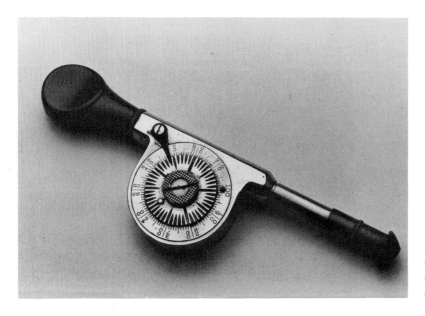

Illus. 148. This antique speed gauge is used to determine the correct speed for any turning operation.

If the spindle is too loose between centers, it will usually rattle a bit, but if for some reason it is so loose that it barely touches the centers, it will just fall onto the bed of the lathe when the machine is turned on.

If the rest is improperly adjusted too closely to the wood, it will create a clatter as it touches the high spot of the wood on each revolution. But if the rest is very close it will stop the spindle dead in its tracks, the V-belt on the pulley will slip, and the spindle will remain stationary until the motor is shut off and the tool rest adjusted out of the way. Don't try to readjust the tool rest with the machine still running. If the rest is just barely touching, tap it with the heel of your hand to help it clear. This should be attempted only by those who are very comfortable with the machine.

Very high speeds may create a great deal of lathe shimmy, and it can literally dance across the floor. This is likely to happen when turning off-center pieces. Stop the lathe and reduce the speed.

The last area to watch is the space between the tool rest and the wood. This constitutes a possible pinch point if you catch the heel of your hand while the wood is turning. Ordinarily, your hand would not be there unless you were trying to stop the turning from spinning after the motor was turned off. The wound from the friction burn heals quickly and is mostly embarrassing.

Of course, don't wear anything loose that can get caught in the revolving work. If turning is a formal occasion, wear a bow tie.

Cylinder-making Technique

Roughing out. The first step in cutting the rough square of wood is to reduce it to a cylinder. The tool designed to do this is the roughing gouge. When preparing to use the roughing gouge, it is a good idea to position the tool rest about 1 in. (25 mm) longer than the end that is turned first (Illus. 149). Cuts can then be made at the ends without running off the tool rest. It is possible to use a much longer tool rest for longer turnings, which will make the work of reducing the size of the cylinder more continuous. It takes too much time to set up a special tool-rest base and to go through the tightening process just for roughing out. I prefer to cut out as much as possible with the tool rest in position, and then move it along the turning to cut out the rest. The roughing gouge is used in a position as close as possible to a right angle to the axis of the work (Illus.

150). Thus, by going straight into the wood with the tool, both sides of the gouge are used and the fibres of the wood are scored at the same time. The roughing gouge is an extremely safe tool, and it is almost impossible to do something dangerous, so a little angling to the side won't hurt.

Hand position is the next important consideration. The hand holding the handle is the depth regulator and must be near the end of the handle for good leverage. The other hand guides the tool along the tool rest. There are two possible positions for this hand. The first is resting it on top of the tool an inch (25 mm) or so away from the edge of the blade. The second is gripping the tool from the bottom of the blade and resting the index finger against the tool-rest casting. I prefer the first method because it is more comfortable to rest my hand on top and use its weight to keep the tool in position. With the second method, I must hold up my hand and this is more tiring than resting it on top.

To begin the cut, turn on the lathe, and with the handle well down and the bottom of the gouge sitting on the top of the tool rest, allow the bevel to rub on the wood. This puts the cutting edge of the tool in a much higher position than normally needed for cutting but it is a good place to start. Next raise the handle until the edge begins to cut. Hold the tool firmly enough on the rest to control it, but not so firmly that it is difficult to adjust the tool and movements become jerky. At the start of this reducing process, it is a good idea to take light cuts and remove only the very corners of the square of wood. Too deep a cut at this point runs the risk of chipping out a larger piece than bargained for. Move the gouge along the rest in a smooth, fluid motion (Illus. 151). By swaying your entire

Illus. 149. Position the tool rest at least 1 in. (25 mm) longer than the end of the cylinder you are roughing out.

Illus. 150. Position the roughing gouge at a right angle to the axis of the wooden blank.

149

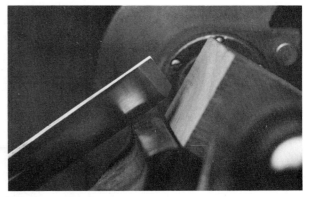

150

Illus. 151a–c. For the roughing cut, move the gouge along the tool rest in a smooth fluid motion.

151a

151b

151c

body with the cut, it will be easier to maintain the same approximate edge position throughout the cut. It's fine to move back and forth laterally during this cut. After the high points of the corners have been removed by a series of light cuts, lift up a bit more on the handle, push in a bit more, and take a deeper bite into the wood. Continue to make these cuts until you reach the largest diameter needed for the turning, which can be checked with a pair of calipers.

In the process of making these roughing cuts, the high points will become identifiable by a translucent shadow on the top surface of the revolving wood. As this shadow is reduced the cylindrical shape will gradually become evident. Test this surface, after much of the material has been removed, by touching the top of the revolving wood lightly with the palm of your hand. The alternative method is to turn off the lathe and revolve the wood by hand to find any remaining high spots.

While you are removing more and more wood the distance between the tool rest and the wood becomes greater. If the distance is ½ in. (13 mm) or so, you won't need to stop the lathe and move the rest closer. But more than that and you probably should move it. Because the roughing gouge is very strong, even a ¾-in. (19-mm) extension over the tool rest would not present a dangerous situation.

It is usually a good idea to make one final pass on the wood to smooth out some of the high ridges before going on to the next step. Do this with the side of the gouge. Hold the tool again at a right angle to the wood's axis, rub the bevel on the wood, and with the shallower side edge of the blade slowly move it along the tool rest to make a fine, controlled cut (Illus. 152). Both sides of the

Illus. 152. After roughing out, smooth out the high ridges with the side edge of the gouge.

gouges are much shallower than the center section; use either for this smoothing cut. Moving at a moderate speed will make possible the removal of the high spots; moving too fast will likely create a new set of ridges.

Steps for roughing out:

- ☐ Place the tool rest as close as possible to the wood.
- ☐ Turn on the lathe.
- ☐ Position the blade of the roughing gouge on the tool rest perpendicular to the axis of the wood with the handle low and the cutting end moderately high.
- ☐ Allow the bevel of the blade to lightly rub the wood and lift the handle slowly until only the corners of the wood are being removed.
- ☐ Slide the blade along the tool rest from side to side making even cuts.
- ☐ Continue to move the blade along the tool rest taking deeper cuts and moving the tool rest closer to the wood as necessary until the predetermined diameter is reached.
- ☐ Make one or more smoothing cuts with either shallow side of the cutting edge.

Marking out. After the cylinder has been cut, the next step is to mark it in some way for further detailing or decorating. For this operation, there are several ways to mark both the areas for decoration and their approximate diameters. For the first method, assuming that we are following a blueprint of the design, use a ruler and pencil to mark the spacing and the widths of the decorative elements directly onto the spindle (Illus. 153). Place the tool rest close to the work and place the ruler on top of it. Turn on the lathe and with a pencil mark all of the important landmarks of the proposed turning on the wood. Hold the pencil firmly or lay it on the tool rest so that the mark will go precisely where you want it to go. Another method to mark out landmarks requires a pair of dividers. This is a little slower because the dividers have to be continually reset as you move along the spindle, identifying the width of a cove, for example, by adjusting the dividers to that width directly on the blueprint. Mark the spindle by holding the dividers horizontally on the tool rest and pushing into the revolving wood. For exact measurement, the divider cut is more accurate than the pencil method on the fuzzy roughed wood.

With all of the key elements of the turning now identified on the cylinder, mark out the diameters. A decorated spindle presents a number of different diameters. By establishing these diameters in the beginning, we have a place to work to with chisels and gouges in the next phase. The tool used for this is the parting tool. The parting tool is double-bevelled and chisel-shaped. By placing the cutting edge parallel to the surface of the wood, you can make deep plunging cuts to the desired diameter. The tool is easy to use. With the tool rest positioned close to the wood and ¼ in. (6 mm) or so below the axis of the wood, rest the bevel on the revolving wood (Illus. 154). Position the blade on the rest and lightly place one hand on it; hold the handle low with the other hand. The tool must always be seated on the tool rest before the bevel touches the wood. Failure to do this is the most common cause of tear-outs in the revolving wood (Illus. 155). The tool must be fairly high to start the cut and should slowly arc into the wood with the hand holding the handle controlling the arc (Illus. 156). Keep the tool high and *arc* straight in. Try not to rock the tool during the cut because any rocking will show up as friction and heat. If the tool is held too low and pushed rather than arced straight in, the lovely shavings that are possible will only be powder, and it will be more difficult to make deep cuts.

Steps to remember for using the parting tool:
- ☐ Check the position of the tool rest.
- ☐ Turn on the lathe.
- ☐ Position the blade on the rest with the handle low and the blade end high.
- ☐ Allow the bevel to rub on the wood to start the cut.
- ☐ Slowly lift the handle until shavings appear (if you are getting only powder, the blade edge is too low).
- ☐ Continue to lift the handle, using the tool rest as a fulcrum, and arc the tool into the wood.

This is how the parting tool is used. Practice for a while and make a number of cuts along the length of the roughed-out spindle.

The next exercise is to make these cuts with one hand while determining the diameter with a previously set pair of calipers in the

Illus. 153. One way to mark the spacing and widths of the decorative elements directly onto the spindle is with a ruler and pencil.

Illus. 154. Position the parting tool on the rest as shown, just prior to making the first plunging cut.

Illus. 155. Example of a tear-out caused by an unsupported part of the tool edge catching in the turning wood.

Illus. 156. With the bevel resting on the wood, arc the parting tool into the wood from a fairly high position.

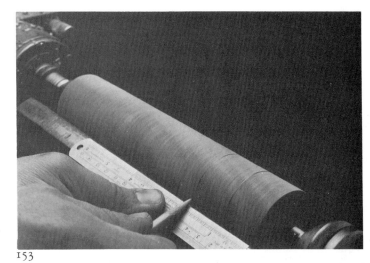

153

155

154

156

other (Illus. 157). It sounds hard but it really isn't. The cut can be made with both hands, if that's more comfortable; the only difference is that the hand normally resting on top of the tool will have to do a little work for a change. Use only calipers with rounded edges because the sharp corners on some cheaper makes catch in the wood and are dangerous. But a little grinding, filing, and polishing can make them clean and usable.

To make the cut, hold the parting tool somewhere in the middle on the blade where it joins the handle. Put the tool on the rest in the same position as that used with both hands. The calipers are held at the top around the spring mechanism and positioned over the spindle. Keep your elbow up and clear of the spindle. When you start to make the cut with the tool edge held high there will be the usual resistance to the cut, which is a little harder to overcome because there is only one hand to counteract it. Adjust the tool down a little bit to reduce the resistance, but not so low that you are again removing powder that looks more like baking soda than wood. If the result is more like baking soda, you might as well be using sandpaper. After the initial incision into the wood, the resistance quickly fades; now arc the tool into the wood. Place the calipers held in the other hand right in the cut as soon as you make it and continue to rub against the wood with the calipers until the preset diameter is reached. At this point, the calipers will slide over the spindle. The

Illus. 157. Make depth cuts with the parting tool. Simultaneously, hold calipers in the cut to signal that the predetermined diameter has been reached, at which point they will slip over the wood.

round edges help the calipers slide; just pull them back and off the turning. The whole motion of cutting and measuring happens so quickly that after you've done it a few times, it will become fluid and second nature.

The woodturner's sizing tool (Illus. 158), when used with a series of side-by-side parting-tool cuts at the end of the spindle, will make a tenon. The tenon is the part of the spindle that is formed into a small cylindrical end and fits into a seat bottom. The sizing tool is

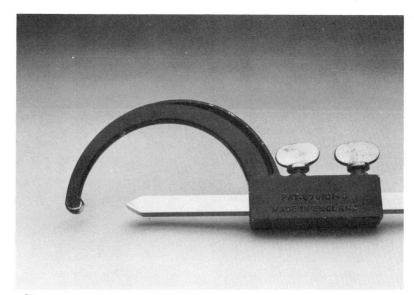

158a

Illus. 158. (a) Modern and (b) antique woodturner's sizing tools are used to make a tenon at the end of a spindle.

158b

both a holder for the parting tool and a caliper all in one. An adjustment in the sizing tool in or out will effectively change the diameter that the parting tool will automatically cut. The tool is easy to set. Use a ruler to set the distance between the cutting edge and the rounded end of the caliper leg (Illus. 159) so that it is equivalent to the diameter desired. Arc the tool into the wood in the same way as you would with the parting tool (Illus. 160). When the preset diameter is reached, the wood will fit through the opening between the rounded caliper end and the cutting edge. This method is very fast

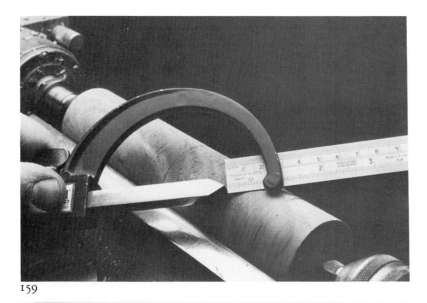

159

160

Illus. 159. A ruler is used to set the distance between the cutting edge of the parting tool and the rounded end of the caliper leg so that the equivalent diameter is cut on the spindle.

Illus. 160. Cutting with the sizing tool. When the preset diameter is reached, the wood fits between the caliper end and the cutting edge of the tool.

for making successive side-by-side cuts for tenons, but for depth cuts along the length of the spindle I prefer to use the thinner parting tool and a pair of calipers. The latter method produces a narrower cut quicker, and the thickness of the leg does not get in the way.

Planing the cylinder and cone. The neatest way to make cylindrical or cone shapes on some spindle designs is to use either a skew or square chisel. The chisel on such a surface is like a smoothing plane on a table top; it is possible to leave a shiny, blemish-free surface.

To make the planing cut for a cylinder use only the center of the edge; the corners of the tool must not touch the wood. The square-across chisel is the easiest tool to use because it is not awkward to get the tool into the right position to make the cut. Before starting the cut, first check the position of the tool rest. It should be high and close to the wood. Raise the tool rest almost to the top of the spindle (Illus. 161). In fact it may have to go lower if the shaft on the tool rest is not long enough. The purpose in raising the tool rest that high is to make it easier to control the skimming cut on the top of the spindle, more comfortable for you to hold the tool, and easier to see what you are doing. It is also important that the top of the tool rest be smooth so that there will be no obstruction to the fluid movement of the tool.

Next turn on the lathe, and with the handle low, lay the blade of the chisel on the tool rest at an angle that approximates a shearing

Illus. 161. When planing a cylinder, position the tool rest slightly lower than the top of the spindle.

position in line with the grain of the wood (Illus. 162). Now lift the handle until the bevel, but not the cutting edge, is resting directly on the wood (Illus. 163). This is not as difficult as it may seem, and it is important that the cutting edge of the tool does not touch the wood until the edge is adjusted so that only the center can cut the wood. It will be possible to see if the bevel is rubbing properly on the wood. As noted previously, the handle is the depth-of-cut regulator, so raise it until fine and small shavings are made (Illus. 164). One important point to remember is to start any cut ¾ in. (19 mm) or so from the end of the blank. In this way, rest the bevel firmly on the top of the wood, and this support is the key to the cut, far more important than the support of the tool on the tool rest. The hand holding the blade can be rested on the top of the tool or on the bottom, whichever is more comfortable to make the controlled cut. It often helps to glide the heel of the hand or the index finger along the ridge on the tool rest, guiding the movement of the tool.

The angle of the cutting edge is variable. The important thing is to cut only with the center section of the tool. In the beginning it is good to use a greater angle in relation to the axis of the wood for the cut. This makes smaller shavings, but it is easier to control when learning how to make the cut. After gaining more confidence, use a smaller angle so that more edge will be in contact with the wood, and it will be easier to make a smooth and flat surface. The high po-

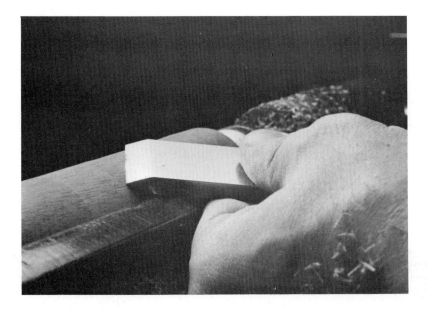

Illus. 162. When planing a cylinder, place the blade of the chisel in line with the grain of the wood, approximating a shearing position.

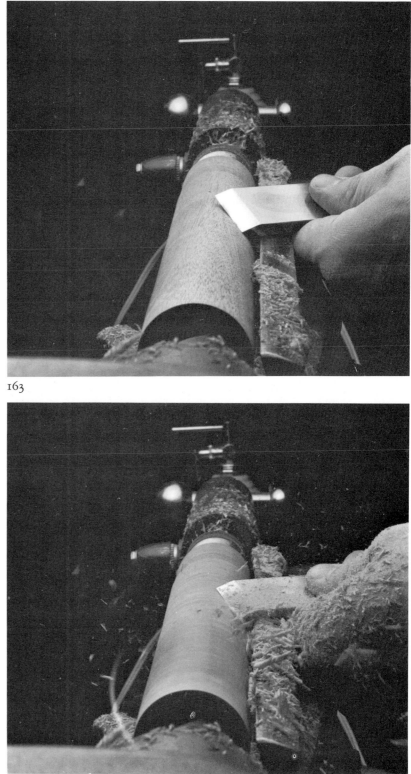

163

164

Illus. 163. Prior to making the planing cut, rest the bevel of the chisel on the wood.

Illus. 164. Slowly raise the handle of the chisel from the bevel resting position until fine and small shavings are planed from the cylinder.

sition of the rest facilitates both observation of the shavings curling over the top of the edge and adjustment of the angle so that the corners of the tool are away from the wood.

If the wood still has a number of ridges left from the gouge, you will have to remove them before the entire surface can be planed smooth (Illus. 165). This type of cut is also easy if the bevel is used as a fulcrum; rock the bevel against the wood until only the tops of the ridges are being cut off (Illus. 166). Thus, the adjusted position of the edge allows the bevel to ride on the low points along the spindle, while the edge cuts the high points. Hold the tool in the same position during the cut completely along the length of the spindle. This is important because of the natural tendency to follow the contours of the roughed-out blank. Use the tool rest and hold hands and arms in the same position throughout the cut. After the high areas have been removed, you will be able to plane the entire surface (Illus. 167).

One final note on keeping the corners away from the wood. The lower corner or the corner nearest to the tool rest is the least problem. If it digs into the wood it is still supported on the rest, but the cut will be deeper as the tool plows through the wood. However, if the other corner catches in the wood, it is unsupported on the rest and will cause the tool to slam down on the rest. When the outside corner catches in the wood, it also tears it out, and this usually ruins the piece or at least causes a quick design change.

The only remaining cut to practice is the one used to remove the wood from the end of the spindle. Starting just inside the end of the spindle means that there will be a high spot or larger diameter at one end. The safest way to remove this is by reversing the tool so that the handle is on the opposite side of your body, and the handle is in the other hand. Move your entire body with the cutting edge towards that uncut end. Practice this with the machine turned off so that the moves become familiar and turn the machine on only when you are absolutely comfortable using the other hand.

Steps to remember for planing the cylinder:
☐ Position the tool rest almost as high as the top of the spindle.
☐ Place the tool rest close to the spindle and check that there are no obstructions by rotating the wood.
☐ Turn on the lathe and lay the blade of the tool on the tool rest ¾ in. (19 mm) inside the end of the spindle.

Illus. 165. Remove any ridges left by the roughing gouge before planing the cylinder smooth.

Illus. 166. Ridges left by the roughing gouge can be seen on the turning wood. The bevel of the chisel is used as a fulcrum and rocked against the wood until only the tops of the ridges are being cut off.

Illus. 167. After the ridges are removed, the cylinder is ready for the final planing.

165

166

167

- ☐ Lift the handle until the bevel is rubbing on the wood and adjust the angle of the blade so that the center of the bevel is on the wood.
- ☐ Lift the handle a bit more so that the cutting edge begins to cut finely.
- ☐ Guide the cut with the heel or index finger of the hand holding the blade riding along the ridge of the tool rest.
- ☐ Control the cut by swaying laterally with your whole body in a fluid movement along the length of the spindle.
- ☐ Use the bevel as a fulcrum to adjust the depth of cut for removing ridges left by roughing out.

Planing the cone shape. With some practice, you will find that by holding the blade very firmly on the tool rest, you can take deeper planing cuts and still leave a burnished surface. The process for making a cone shape is very similar to that for making a cylinder. To start, it's a good idea to make depth cuts along the length of the spindle with a parting tool (Illus. 168) to mark the angle desired for the cone. The parting cuts, made with a caliper, should not cut down to the cone's final depth, because it is preferable to give oneself an allowance for final planing cuts. The procedure for planing the cone shape is the same as that for the cylinder. The difference is that you should continuously lift the handle throughout the cut in a smooth even motion that matches the shape of the cone. It is necessary to make a series of shallow planing cuts between the already established depth cuts (Illus. 169) until you reach the shape that you want. Although these first cuts will be coarse, the final cut will be the smoothing cut and will determine the surface finish. If the planed cone shape ends in a shoulder or in a design element that has a larger diameter, it will be necessary to angle the edge of the chisel to a perpendicular position to finish the cut. For this type of operation, I prefer to use a skew chisel. At that angle, a square-across chisel would be impossible to support on the tool rest.

This seems like a good point to mention the finesse and care required when handling chisels and turning tools in general. Make conscious movements with the tools. It seems that problems always happen when a careless move is made. Lack of concentration is probably the most common fault and cause of dig-ins. For example, while planing a cylinder you may feel like backtracking to clean up an area

Illus. 168. The cone shape is initially determined by depth cuts made with a parting tool along the length of the spindle.

Illus. 169. Make a series of shallow planing cuts between the depth cuts until the cone shape is reached.

168

169

just passed that wasn't cut properly. Unfortunately, you run the risk of catching the edge in the spindle. When moving forward with the cut, you can force the edge of the blade down on the wood by the shaving on the top of the bevel. This action does not occur when the tool is pulled backwards. The controlled, deliberate series of movements outlined earlier for putting tool to rest, bevel to wood, and edge to wood should be practiced and followed exactly until the movements become graceful, fluid, and second nature.

Steps for making and planing the cone shape:

☐ Position the tool rest below the axis of the wood.

☐ Using the parting tool and calipers make a series of oversized cuts along the length of the cone that correspond to predetermined diameters for the cone.

☐ Position the tool rest almost as high as the top of the spindle.

☐ Lay the blade of the tool on the tool rest at one end of the cone shape.

☐ Lift the handle until the bevel is rubbing on the wood and adjust the angle of the blade so that the center of the bevel is on the wood.

☐ Lift the handle a bit more so that the cutting edge begins to cut finely.

☐ Guide the cut with the heel or index finger of the hand holding the blade riding along the ridge of the tool rest.

☐ Working from the larger to the smaller diameter, lift the handle progressively higher taking deeper cuts and matching the predetermined cone shape. Be sure that only the center part of the edge is contacting the wood for these cuts.

☐ After making these coarse cuts, make one final controlled pass to smooth the surface of the cone.

Cove or hollow. Every hollow shape made for decorative effect on a spindle is a derivative of the cove. The tools designed for making the cove are the spindle gouges. They are shallow gouges, at least shallower than the deeper roughing or bowl gouges, and have a cutting edge shaped like a ladyfinger. It is the sides of the spindle gouge's edge that are relied on for most of the cutting action. The first steps in making the cove are to mark the width of the cove and make the depth cut with the parting tool. The depth cut made with a parting tool and caliper establishes the cove's minimum diameter, and the divider marks identify the cove's width.

To begin the cut, lower the tool rest from the high position it was in when planing with the chisel. A little below the center line of the spindle is a good place to start but feel free to lower it a bit more to accommodate the height of the lathe, size of the spindle, and the length of the bevel on the gouge. You must be comfortable at the machine in order to have full control of the cuts, so if any doubt exists when beginning to position the tool and practice the cuts, experiment with the height of the tool rest.

The principles of cutting with the spindle gouge are the same as with all other cutting tools: position the tool on the rest, rub the bevel on the wood, and cut from a larger diameter to a smaller diameter. To start the cove shape, place the blade on the tool rest with the handle moderately low and the blade extended over the rest high enough so that the side of the edge will be in position to start the cut (Illus. 170). It's best to begin near the parting-tool cut. With the blade resting on its side and the hollow of the gouge facing the parting-tool cut, make the cut by lifting the handle until the lower part of the cutting edge pierces the wood (Illus. 171). There are a couple of ways to make this first piercing cut: one is to arc the edge down slowly but firmly, and the other is to nearly push the tool in straight.

Once the tool is in the wood, make a rolling movement with the tool handle while advancing into the wood. The advancing and rolling action occur at the same time, and they must proceed so that at the end of the cut when it reaches the bottom of the cove shape, the hollow in the tool is facing up (Illus. 172). Little wood will be removed for these first cuts, so the rolling and advancing will not be dramatic. At this stage, however, it is important to make a sweep on each side of the parting-tool cut. By removing the same amount from each side of the cut, you eliminate the risk of catching the corner of the tool on what is the uphill side of the cove shape.

The movement is the same on the left side of the parting cut as on the right. Lay the blade on its side with the inside hollow facing the depth cut, pierce the wood with the part of the blade near the nose, and make the rolling cut using the upper half of the side-cutting edge to the center point of the cove. The rolling movement is important to make the desired fair, round shape. If the bevel is not rubbing properly and the cut is made with the nose instead of rolling from the nose to the center of the side edge, the surface will have a number of ridges. The area where the bevel was rubbing and where it stopped rubbing will be visible by the placement of the ridges. If ridges appear and the surface becomes more flat than round, it is usually because you are making an improper scooping motion. Turn off the lathe and practice the motion. Probably the tool edge is very close to the tool rest; move it out further so that you can use more of the side of the cutting edge.

170

171

172

Illus. 170. To begin the cove shape, extend the blade of the spindle gouge over the tool rest high enough so that the side of the edge will be in position to start the cut.

Illus. 171. With the blade resting on its side and the hollow of the gouge facing the parting tool cut, lift the handle until the lower part of the cutting edge pierces the wood.

Illus. 172. Once the tool is in the wood, make a rolling movement with the tool handle while advancing into the wood, so that at the end of the cut at the bottom of the cove shape, the hollow of the gouge is facing up.

When the width of the cove was marked out, either with a pencil or with a cut line, the final dimensions for that detail were established. After removing some of the waste from the center of the cove, place the tool on its side, make an incision at the line and roll the cut into the cove. When completed on both sides of the cove, a fence for future cuts is established. Each cut after this can be started with the bevel rubbing against this hollowed out surface just inside of the first cut. This facilitates the start of future cuts because once the bevel is rubbing, only an adjustment of the tool handle is necessary for the depth of cut.

After nearly all of the wood is removed from the center of the cove, make one or two finishing cuts. These should be highly controlled cuts that leave the surface smooth enough to reflect the shiny bevel of the tool. If the initial cuts left the shape of the cove reasonably round, then the finishing cuts will be easy. Take a fine cut from the wood and ride the bevel along the surface as a guide.

There are times when longer and broader hollows will be needed. After roughing out the shape with the parting tool and the gouge, turn the tool more on its underside with the hollow facing up and use more of the bevel and the nose for cutting. The initial cuts require a firmer grip because more of the wood is removed with this part of the edge, but the final smoothing cut, with the entire bevel rubbing, will be easy.

If making the cove without first making depth cuts with the parting tool, start the roughing out with a gouge cut using the nose of the cutting edge and removing wood in the center of the future cove. After removing only a little from this area, begin with the rolling cut.

The only dangerous problems possible when using the gouge are in touching the cutting edge to the wood before it touches the tool rest, or in trying to cut uphill. The first is easy to understand, but the second may not be evident even when it happens. When the gouge is used to hollow out a cove, it is rolling down from a larger diameter to a smaller diameter. Because the bottom of the blade is round, it matches the rounded shape of the cutting edge and gives it good support on the tool rest. If at the bottom of the cove you continue on up the other side, essentially working uphill, two parts of the edge will be touching the wood but only one of them will be supported by the tool rest. Because the wood is turning towards you, the natural reaction is for the wood to catch the unsupported edge section and push it down onto the tool rest. This results in a lovely spiral tear that needs cleaning up. The problem is more frightening than dangerous. It usually happens because of carelessness or fatigue. If the tear-out happens at the beginning of the hollowing process in the cove, then there is some waste left to remove, and it is possible to get below the tear-out.

One final word about using spindle gouges concerns the size necessary for a desired cut. In general, use a gouge that is about half the size of the final width of the cove. For example, to make a ¾- or a 1-in. (19- or a 25-mm)-wide cove use a ⅜-in. (10-mm) gouge. The measurement need not be precise, but if the gouge is too small there will not be enough bevel on the wood to make a controlled cut. If the gouge is too big, it will literally get buried in the cut, and it might get caught on the other side of the cove.

Steps for making the cove:

☐ Position the tool rest a little below the center line and close to the spindle.

☐ Turn on the lathe.

☐ Place the blade of the gouge on the tool rest with the handle moderately low and the blade extended over the rest high enough so that the side of the edge will be in position to start the cut.

☐ With the blade resting on its side and the hollow of the gouge facing the parting-tool cut, make the cut by lifting the handle until the lower part of the cutting edge pierces the wood.

☐ Continue the cut by advancing the edge into the wood and rolling the tool so that by the end of the cut the hollow of the blade will be facing up. Resist the temptation to cut uphill.

☐ Using the opposite side of the tool edge, make the same advancing and rolling movement to hollow the opposite side of the cove.

☐ After establishing the full width and diameter of the cove with roughing cuts, make a final finishing cut by using the lower part of the cutting edge nearer the nose and starting the cut just inside the preceding roughing cut. The finishing cut should be slow and even to remove all ridges left by roughing cuts.

☐ Using the opposite side of the tool edge, make the finishing cut on the opposite side of the cove.

Bead or rounding over. The opposite shape to the cove is the bead, and in many ways the method of making it is similar to that used for making the cove. Again, the spindle gouge is used, but for the bead the smallest gouge, the ¼-in. (6-mm) gouge, is used. This small gouge is well suited to the task because on most beads the amount of wood to be removed is very small. In addition, contacting the wood with only a small amount of bevel and cutting edge leaves a smooth surface. Rounding over constitutes a shearing across the end grain and uses an extremely shallow part of the cutting edge. For larger beads and round surfaces switch to the ⅜-in. (10-mm) spindle gouge because the work will go more quickly using a slightly larger blade even though a small amount of the edge is actually doing the cutting.

To start, mark out the width of the proposed bead and make a couple of cuts with the parting tool and calipers to establish the proposed diameter on each side of the bead. This will leave a squared section in the center for making the bead. Position the tool rest close to the work, lower than the axis of the spindle. Turn the lathe on and place the tool on the tool rest with the hollow slightly rocked over towards the parting cut (Illus. 173). The part of the edge near the nose is used to round over the square on each side. Be sure that the tool is extended out enough on the rest and begin by shaving off the corner of the square. It's best to start at the corner, and with each successive cut increase the rounded shape. As usual, proceed from the largest diameter to the smallest, and don't try to work uphill or a dig-in might result. As with the cove cuts, the bevel rubs on the wood to adjust edge position and the edge rolls in the cut, while the blade is supported on the tool rest. The handle in this case must roll in a way that mimics the desired shape. This rolling action is achieved by raising the handle slightly throughout the cut and twisting the handle in your hand in an overhand sort of way. The hand holding the blade is there primarily for support and enables the blade to follow through the cut smoothly. It is this smoothness of blade action that results in a smooth surface. For those who are right-handed, the tool will be positioned by your right side. To make the cut on the opposite side of the bead either switch hands and do the cut left-handed or move over and approach the left side of the bead with the other side of the blade. Use the same rolling action and follow through while cutting with the edge of the blade near the nose as it rests on its side.

173a

173b

173c

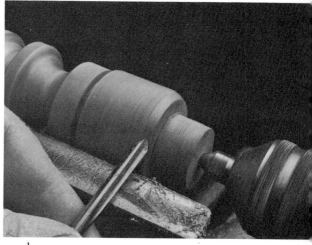

173d

173e

Illus. 173a–e. Sequence of movements to make a rolling cut for a beading or rounding-over element. Proceeding from the largest to the smallest diameter with the hollow of the gouge slightly rocked over towards the parting cut, use a rolling motion to round over the square with the edge near the nose of the gouge.

Use some finesse when making this cut. If the rolling action on either side of the bead is not smooth, the result may be either a flat or hollow surface. Also follow through with the cut. Don't stop the cut before getting near the bottom or you will produce a small ridge there. To remove the ridge, hold the tool firmly on the next pass and plow through it.

After making the initial roughing and rounding cuts, make the final finishing cut. This is a highly controlled cut and is taken a little slower than the roughing cuts that preceded it. With this cut, as with all cuts, you must remove fine shavings, not powder. If powder is the result, lower the handle and place the cutting tool higher before beginning the cut. It will become apparent, after some practice, that a properly made cut removes practically one continuous spiral of wood. Such a result also represents mastery of the cutting technique. Experiment by moving the handle around a bit at the beginning of the cut in order to penetrate the wood precisely; but having achieved this, try to follow that depth throughout the cut.

Steps for making the bead with the spindle gouge:
- ☐ Position the tool rest a little below the center line and close to the spindle.
- ☐ Turn on the lathe.
- ☐ Place the tool on the tool rest with the hollow of the gouge slightly rocked over towards the parting cut.
- ☐ Using the part of the edge nearest the nose, round over the corner by lifting the handle and rolling the tool from the larger to the smaller diameter with the bevel rubbing the wood until the hollow of the gouge faces directly into the parting cut.
- ☐ Using the opposite edge of the tool near the nose, follow the same procedure to round over the corner of the opposite side of the bead.

Another tool used to round over is the skew chisel (Illus. 174). For this cut use the short corner of the cutting edge. This corner penetrates the wood initially with only a small amount of the bevel near it rubbing on the wood. As usual, the blade should be positioned on the tool rest, the handle should be down, and the tool should be extended out over the rest before making the cut. The critical part of the cut is in the penetration of the point into the wood. To do this, you must angle the cutting edge in relation to the wood so that the point alone slices off the corner. The handle must

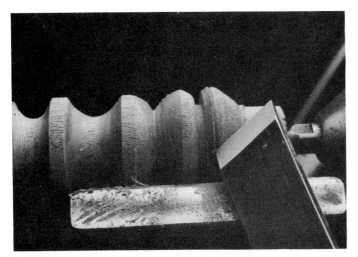

Illus. 174a–c. Rounding over with the skew chisel. Using only the point of the short corner of the cutting edge, roll the handle through the cut in the same way as when rounding with the gouge.

174a

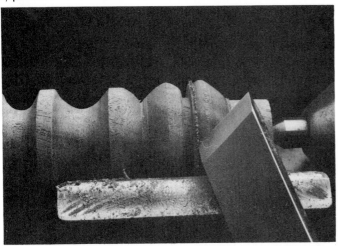

174b

174c

again roll through the cut in the same way as when rounding with the gouge, because to control the depth of cut the bevel near the point must roll through the cut by rubbing on the wood just behind the point. This time, however, since a chisel blade is flat and one corner is positioned on the tool rest, the handle must be lifted as it rolls into the cut in a slicing motion. The rounding on the other side is achieved in the same way but with the point turned in the opposite direction.

The most common problem in learning this technique is letting too much of the cutting edge near the point engage the wood. Too much wood is thereby removed, and part of the blade touches the wood unsupported by the rest, resulting in a possible tear-out. Instead of a round shape, a flat area develops where the broad edge cut. Another problem is not touching enough of the blade to the wood. If only the point but no part of the bevel rubs the wood, the surface cut will be a series of ridges. The point in this case is being allowed to do what it wants to with little depth of cut. Both of these problems are common in the beginning, but there is a way to overcome them. It all happens in the beginning of the cut. After penetrating the wood with the point, adjust the handle to rest the bevel near the point on the wood. This is a slight movement. You must see only the smallest wedge near the point buried in the cut. If more of the blade is cutting, twist it out again slightly. This manœuvring helps establish the depth of cut, after which you can practice control by keeping it there throughout the cut. The shaving must come off in one continuous peeling, like an onion skin. It will take a bit of practice to achieve finesse in this technique and to achieve the shape desired.

Which tool is best for this kind of cut—the gouge or the short corner of the skew chisel? Actually the choice will depend on which tool is either sharper or handier. Increased dexterity with all of the tools will mean making cuts with whatever is closest or already in hand. The skew chisel has always been the favorite of the professional turner because of its wide range of possible cuts, but many have found that the gouge is easier to use. The choice is up to you.

Steps for making a bead with the skew chisel:
- ☐ Position the tool rest a little below the center line and close to the spindle.
- ☐ Turn on the lathe.

□ Place the blade of the chisel on the tool rest so that the short corner of the edge can be used to penetrate the wood.

□ With the handle down and the blade slightly rocked away from the direction of the cut, slowly lift the handle while penetrating the wood with the short corner of the edge in a slicing and rolling movement.

□ Only ⅛ in. (3 mm) or so of the corner should be allowed to penetrate the wood in making the cut.

□ Repeat the slicing and rolling movement on the opposite side of the bead using the same short corner of the edge.

The last tool used for making beading cuts is called the beading tool. It was common in the past for turners to use it to make beads of small to moderate size. The tool has a double-bevelled square end, and in practice its corners are used in exactly the same way as the corner on the skew chisel, but each corner can be used for opposite sides of the bead.

Before finishing off with the beading cut I want to emphasize two things. First, the motor speed used when making the beading cuts or cove cuts must be high; too slow, and you will not be able to get a smooth, burnished surface. Also, it is more difficult to make the first penetrating cuts into the wood at a slower motor speed. Second, it is very important to tune up the edges of the skew chisel blade, using methods explained earlier, and to polish the tool rest. Failure to follow these two rules is instrumental in hampering most beginning turners.

Square cut or facing off. End grain is the terror of all woodturners. All of the techniques discussed depend on the shearing cut to slice end grain, thus eliminating sanding. End grain is particularly exposed at the square cut, typically at a shoulder near a tenon. This is not the only place where it occurs. It will be found to varying degrees on other details.

To cut end grain you must use the long point of the skew chisel. The tool rest should be positioned slightly below the axis of the spindle. To make the cut, place the long side of the chisel blade on the tool rest with the bevel perpendicular to the axis of the spindle (Illus. 175). Keep the blade high at the start and rub the bevel along the end grain of the wood in the direction desired for the cut. Begin

Illus. 175a,b. Sequence of movements to make a facing off or square cut. Begin the cut by arcing into the perimeter of the parting cut with the long, sharp point of the skew chisel. Taking off only a thin sliver of wood at a time, use the tool rest as a fulcrum and slice down to the correct depth.

175a

175b

the cut by penetrating the perimeter of the wood with the long, sharp point of the skew. Take off only a thin sliver of the wood at a time, so that full control will be maintained without great exertion. If the bevel is perpendicular and the tool is high enough, you will be able to arc the tool using the tool rest as a fulcrum; then slice down to the depth desired. If the tool is too low, you will have to push rather than arc the tool in, and control will be more difficult to maintain. To make a cut on the opposite side use the other side of the blade with the same technique, but of course move over to accommodate this position.

Common problems encountered in making this cut are known as undercut and overcut. Undercut occurs when the nose of the blade is allowed to go off on its own because the bevel is not perpendicular at the start of the cut or the handle of the tool is angled out during the cut. Overcut happens when the tool handle is angled in towards the body levering the pointed edge of the blade out of a straight line. A well-made arcing slice, made in one continuous cut (Illus. 176), will shine and have no ridges to identify where the cut was stopped and then started again. Look at the cut closely and use a square if necessary to check control. For each cut made, try to remove as little as possible, creating a paper-thin cut. Again, the shaving can be removed in one continuous piece.

Steps for making the square cut with the skew chisel:
- ☐ Position the tool rest a little below the center line and close to the spindle.
- ☐ Turn on the lathe.
- ☐ To make the cut place the long side of the chisel blade on the tool rest with the bevel perpendicular to the axis of the spindle.
- ☐ Penetrate the surface of the spindle with the bevel rubbing the end grain of the wood and the long point arcing down to the desired depth in a slicing movement.
- ☐ Slice only a small shaving of wood at a time for maximum control.

Illus. 176. Sequence of movements for a well-made arcing slice. To make a slice that will shine and have no ridges, use one continuous movement to remove paper-thin shavings. (a) In an accurate approach to the wood the bevel of the blade is perpendicular to the spindle axis. (b) This angle of approach is too acute to the spindle axis; the resulting cut will be either a series of ridges or a hollow undercut. (c) This angle of approach to the spindle is too obtuse and will result in an irregular cone shape.

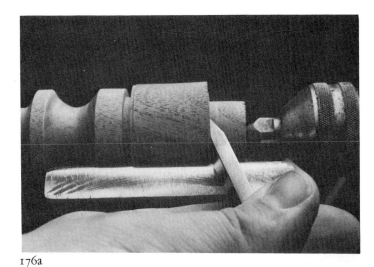

176a

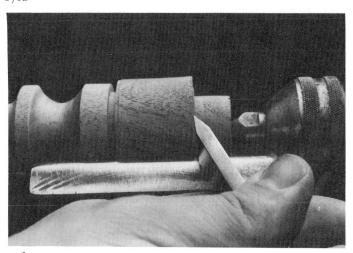

176b

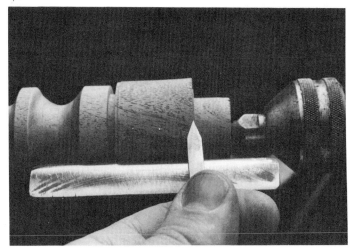

176c

VI · Vessel, or Faceplate, Turning

*V*essel turning is the craft of turning hollow forms. Bowls, platters, and containers fall into this category. It is often called faceplate turning, but the availability of diverse holding devices and the common use of the tailstock to hold wood during vessel turning makes that name less accurate than it once was.

The grain direction of vessels is usually face grain. That is, the grain direction on the top or bottom of the vessel is long grain from side to side, versus end grain and cross grain that are found on spindles. On the exterior and interior of a vessel the grain changes from end grain to edge grain as it turns. This constantly changing grain pattern has some inherent problems and by its nature is more difficult to tame than the more predictable long grain on the spindle. It requires different approaches to cutting and sanding than are used for spindle work. Reliance is placed on the bowl gouge, scrapers, and the disc sander, all of which will be explained in the sections that follow.

As kitchen containers for wet and dry foods in general, vessels in wood have been largely superseded by those in glass and ceramic. Today, wooden bowls are used most often for salad and as centerpieces on tables for holding fruit and other foods. The broad surface of the vessel is still the one preferred by turners to show off and celebrate the beauty of exotic grain patterns and figures in wood. For that reason such items continue to be made by amateurs and professionals alike.

Technique Imperatives

Bowl turning is probably the most popular area of turning today since a finished piece can be produced completely on the lathe with no additional operations. Spindles, on the other hand, are usually components of larger pieces. For example, turning the legs for a gate-leg table represents a single element in a complex and time-consuming project. Thus, both the professional turner and the hobbyist can view bowl turning as a more efficient and gratifying use of their time. But whether or not time is a consideration, the speed in re-moving waste wood afforded by proper technique does bring closer the creative element of shaping the piece.

The critical element in classic bowl-turning technique is a smooth surface; there should be no indication that the piece was scraped, cut, or abraded into shape. Ridges from cutting and scraping tools or broken grain from abrasives are unacceptable. The feel must be silky, just as with any piece of fine furniture. Of course, a certain amount of technical skill is needed to achieve this finish. An experienced viewer will not be deceived by layers of shellac that try to hide a poorly prepared surface. Touching must also reveal smooth, fair lines without bumps made by uncontrolled or erratic tool use. Fingers drawn from the bottom to the edge should be able to move in one continuous sweep, both on the outside and the inside. Hands be-come the calipers that pinch the bowl between index finger and thumb. In many ways, the outside and the inside of the bowl func-tion independently of each other; pleasing shadows play upon both. Although the outside is enjoyed for its three-dimensional qualities, the inside is more two-dimensional, particularly under the flattening light that usually prevails.

Elegance in a bowl is often achieved by making it lightweight. Vessel turnings with most of their interior wood removed can defy their perceived weight and mass. Elegance can also be achieved by il-lusion. A thinly tapered edge, for instance, can belie the thicker wall below it, making the bowl appear lightweight (Illus. 177). And set-ting a large bowl on a small foot or a pedestal (Illus. 178) gives the bowl an appearance of weightlessness, hovering in mid-air.

Illus. 178. An illusion of hovering in mid-air is created by placing this bowl on a pedestal.

The bowl's broad surface provides the turner with good space "to paint" with the grain patterns as they are revealed, using his cutting tool to create a specific pattern. A certain amount of forethought is of course necessary before mounting the block on the lathe, but as the raw wood is sliced away, a fair amount of grain is revealed. The experienced turner working with a familiar wood will always find some nuances because each log is different from the last. He must still follow the grain's lead, because as each layer is cut away in this subtractive process, one pattern is lost and another revealed. Restraint, an understanding of the material, and skill, as well as the inherent beauty of the wood, all contribute to the success of the finished piece.

Design Imperatives

Today's vessel-turning guidelines are far more flexible than ever before. Because vessels are increasingly used as ceremonial and decorative furnishings, their design, surface treatment, weight, thickness, and function can be approached with great freedom. Modern bowls don't have to be smooth, lightweight, have thin translucent walls, or even hold apples. More often today, the vessel documents the exposed beauty of the wood, and rare pieces of wood are handled by the turner with the same reverence as raw diamonds are handled by the diamond cutter. Instead of strictly imposing a design on the wood, the turner "listens" to what the wood has to say: if a grain pattern changes abruptly, the turner's design changes accordingly. This sculptural treatment of the bowl shape must be viewed differently from traditional and functional turning, when designs were executed on the wood regardless of its individual characteristics. Whatever the design, the careful and craftsmanlike handling of the material and the intuitive way of revealing the bowl hidden in the tree remain the essence of woodturning. How turners experiment with various approaches will always be, as it is today, part of the excitement and life of the craft.

The Basic Shape Vocabulary of the Vessel

The following group of simple terms is used in vessel turning to identify the various shapes and products of the craft.

Vessel. The hollow form for holding either wet or dry goods.

Round blank. A disc or block of wood sawed and ready for mounting on the lathe.

Lip. The thin edge (Illus. 179) of a bowl, container lid, vase, etc.

Foot. The integral pedestal (Illus. 180) of a vessel, usually smaller than the body of the vessel itself.

Finial. The spindle-shaped crown (Illus. 181) occasionally used to top off a container lid, grandfather clock, etc.

Illus. 179. The lip of a white oak plate.

Illus. 180. An example of a foot or pedestal on a built-up container.

Illus. 181. A finial of ebony celebrates the chalice shape of this lid.

Any additional terms will be simple and self-explanatory. Some of the terminology used to describe spindle turning also applies to ves-

179

180

181

sel turning. Terms such as bead, cove, and undercut pertain to shapes on vessels as well as spindles.

Vessel-turning Tools

Vessel-turning tools are cutting tools. Although scrapers are used in vessel turning, the small cutting burr formed on the edge of the tool functions as a cutting, not a scraping, instrument. The objective in vessel turning is the same as that in spindle turning, that is, to remove shaving, not powder. In theory, all vessel-turning operations can be accomplished with three tools: the skew scraper, the bowl gouge, and the roundnose scraper (Illus. 182). Smaller scrapers can be added for special detailing but these three make up the basic tool selection. As mentioned in chapter 3 (pages 70–85), the importance of high-speed steel as a tool-making material is much greater for vessel turning than for spindle turning. This is because the bevel of the tool makes contact with the broad surfaces of the vessel for a much longer time, creating more friction and heat (Illus. 183). For the professional turner in particular, it would be very inconvenient to have to remove the tool continually from the cut to cool or resharpen it as the edge is broken down.

A discussion of the characteristics of a range of bowl gouges and scraping tools follows.

Bowl gouge. This tool is unique in its ability to rough out a hollow quickly and also make a fine finishing cut prior to either scraping or sanding. It is possible to obtain the same result with a spindle-turning gouge if the same techniques are followed. The

Illus. 182. The basic tools for vessel turning are the skew scraper, bowl gouge, roundnose finishing scraper, and roundnose roughing scraper.

Illus. 183. The friction and heat produced in vessel turning can render the end of a bowl gouge burned and broken down.

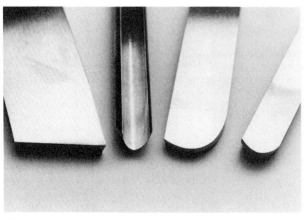

182

183

spindle gouge, however, is not the most efficient tool in this instance because it slows down the cutting.

After completion of all possible cutting with a gouge, the surface must be refined with a scraping tool. The technical ideal would be to rough, shape, and smooth the bowl all with the same gouge. This is usually not possible because the design of the bowl requires scrapers to refine a shape or to make cuts that are not possible with the gouge. It is also necessary to use scrapers for shallow work because such work would be overkill for the larger gouge and is best done with the lighter, more controllable cuts of the scraper. Of course, making a complete bowl is possible with scrapers alone. This is the least appropriate method and extremely time consuming, but the final result—the bowl shape—is all that really matters if time is of no consequence.

As mentioned earlier, scrapers cut with a delicate burr that is formed on the edge of the blade by either grinding or burnishing. This burr looks like a tiny sawtooth edge, and blades of carbon steel are extremely fragile and vulnerable to heat. With high-speed steel, the edge formed is much stronger and resistant to heat. Burnishing, outlined on page 84, is a much better method of establishing a strong, long-lasting burr.

Deep bowl gouge. Until a few years ago, the only bowl gouges available were those designed by Peter and Roy Child. They developed four similarly shaped deep bowl gouges of different widths. The theory was that the largest would be used for the initial roughing out procedure and would be followed by smaller and smaller gouges until the surface was as smooth as possible. This was not smooth enough, however; scraping and sanding were still necessary.

What Peter and Roy Child hoped to design was a bowl gouge that would combine the working characteristics of the set of four gouges. They were successful. Called the Superflute bowl gouge (Illus. 184), it is made of high-speed steel and can withstand friction and heat, unlike the four carbon-steel tools. The Superflute also works because it has a deep center section and high, straight sides (Illus. 185). Thus, it combines the roughing gouge and the chisel into one tool. Wood can be removed quickly, and all of the ridges left by this roughing operation can be removed with the next smoothing cut.

The requirements of the bowl gouge are simple. The profile of the end of the tool must be square across, and the tool must be deep enough to remove the waste quickly. Unfortunately, bowl gouges have often been hard to find in the past, and spindle gouges, although too shallow and not as effective as the bowl gouge, have been made to do their work. Recently, a spindle gouge, called the Stocksdale bowl-turning gouge, has been manufactured. It is made of high-speed steel and completely machined out of round bar stock. The shape is like the spindle gouge because the long curve on the side of the finger shape is deeper than that of a standard spindle gouge. This gouge is more of a finishing tool than a roughing-out tool because it does not remove wood nearly as fast as the deeper bowl gouge.

Roundnose scraper. This scraper features a round-shaped nose (Illus. 186). The sides of the nose are ground back to enhance the tool's side-cutting potential. As a rule, the more rounded the nose, the more useful it is for making roughing cuts that remove large amounts of shavings. Light, refining cuts drawn up the inside of a bowl are made with the long edge ground on the side. Primarily used for hollowing operations on the inside of a bowl, the round-nosed scraper is often used for hollowing or cove-making operations on the outside of the bowl, in creating a foot or pedestal.

Although roundnose scrapers are available in various sizes, thicknesses, and lengths, the thickest tools, measuring ⅜-in. (10-mm), are perfect for burl or spalted wood. Spalted wood is stained brown

Illus. 184. The Superflute bowl gouge combines the working characteristics of four gouges.

Illus. 185. This end view of a Super-flute bowl gouge shows its deep center section and high straight sides.

Illus. 186. The roundnose scraper is primarily used for hollowing operations on the inside of a bowl.

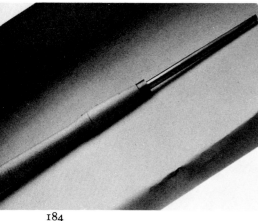

184

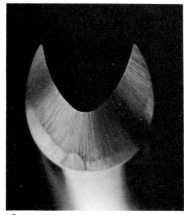

185

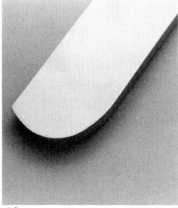

186

and black by fungus, and its structure is compromised by the fungal advance into the wood. This adds an element of uncertainty in turning because the wood is inconsistent, that is, both hard and soft, or punky. With gouges and scrapers it is necessary to keep a steady pressure for cutting both the soft and the hard areas. A heavy, ⅜-in. (10-mm)-thick scraper will absorb vibration and stay put on the rest, thus giving more control. I suppose that a case could be made for this kind of control on nonpunky woods, but I have found the opposite to be true. I have more control with lighter tools in shaping wood of consistent hardness and texture.

The roundnose scraper is a cutting tool capable of removing a lot of wood quickly. Even with the fragile burr, the narrow ¾-in. (19-mm) wide scraper cuts like a gouge. It is considerably slower, however, than the razor-sharp gouge, and the fragile edge is very short-lived, especially when made of carbon steel. Scrapers made of high-speed steel have a much tougher edge and can be used to continue the rough cutting where the gouge left off. The combination of the narrow ¾-in. (19-mm) width and the ⅜-in. (10-mm) thickness make this a fast roughing tool. The narrow width is no help however for the subsequent refining cuts that require a broad, rounded shape to flatten the ridges and produce the fair curves on the rough surface left by the gouge and roughing scraper.

A good width for the smoothing scraper is about 1¼ in. (32 mm), although a 1-in. (25-mm) or 1½-in. (38-mm) scraper can also be used. It is necessary to modify the shape of the edge on any size smoothing scraper. The roundnose finishing scraper in Illus. 182 shows the long edge formed along one side. This is the shape I have found to be the best for making the long sweeping cuts along the bottom and sides of a hollow. I have also ground this shape on my ¾-in. (19-mm) scraper for smoothing smaller hollow shapes.

Square-ended and skew scrapers. These scrapers have straight cutting edges. They can be square across or with the end cutting edge at an angle or skew. These tools can be used interchangeably to flatten the bottom of a bowl or to round over a surface. Certain applications may indicate the use of one over the other and these techniques are covered later on. Standard sizes range from 1 to 1¼ in. (25 to 32 mm). Smaller versions, ranging in size from ⅜ to ½ in. (10 to 13 mm), are available and are used to perform the same functions as the larger tools for more delicate applications.

Side-cutting scraper. When undercutting or boring (scraping straight in), it is sometimes necessary to use a scraper that has a ground or burnished edge on both the side and end of the blade. These are specialized tools available with either a round or flat side-cutting edge. Regrinding an old chisel or scraper to suit a special job is often more practical. Actually, I prefer to use a left-handed skew scraper (Illus. 187) for most applications. On the long corner of the blade I grind a bevel for about 1½ in. (38 mm) of its length. This homemade side cutter is all I need for undercutting and boring of classic plate or bowl forms.

Miniature scrapers. When working with small finials on container lids or other details too large for small gouges and scrapers, it may be necessary to fashion a miniature scraper (Illus. 188). Small, multi-plane grooving cutters, masonry nails, or bench chisels can be ground to the appropriate shape and size to suit a specific application. That way the size of the tool can correspond to the clearance or to the width of the detail that I am making. Carbon steel can be used for these small, lightweight tools although high-speed steel is even better. The light cuts create little heat, and even high-carbon steel will stay sharp.

Carbide-tipped scrapers. An even tougher breed of scraper with carbide-tipped edges is available from suppliers. It is second in hardness to the diamond and very brittle. Carbide is well suited to cutting species of wood high in mineral content or wood with aberrant growth, such as root burls, because it can plow through most obstacles. Brittleness can be a problem, though, and it takes more patience and skill to sharpen carbide. Carbide blanks are available from industrial suppliers, and homemade tools (Illus. 189) can be prepared by silver soldering carbide to mild steel with a portable torch.

Disc sander. The disc sander combined with the reversing switch for the lathe can make turning bowls almost painless. Compared with sanding by hand, this combination probably reduces the chore by two thirds. Two thirds! The problem on all plates or bowls arises from the two areas of end grain on the interior and exterior sides of the form that seem to refuse to be shaved off. Using cutting tools on wood is much the same as shaving hair. As one slices off the top surface of the fibres, the lower portion of the fibres is pushed down in

187

188

189

Illus. 187. Modified skew scraper. The bevel is ground on the long corner of the blade for undercutting and boring of classic plate or bowl forms.

Illus. 188. Set of miniature scrapers for small, detailed operations.

Illus. 189. Homemade carbide-tipped scrapers for turning burls and high-mineral–content wood.

the opposite direction. The reversing switch with the disc sander makes it possible to sand off those pushed down fibres. Disc sanding is described in detail on pages 207–11.

Work-holding Devices

The large group of work-holding devices includes the tools that secure the often ungainly and unbalanced blocks of wood on the lathe while the turner cuts, sands, and finishes. There are many methods for holding wood on the lathe; some are both simple and inexpensive. In just the last few years, the woodturner's chuck has developed from its original status as a custom-made item into a manufactured item. Prior to that time, turners used some less than optimal methods that added an unnecessary element of danger to the practice of turning. Today, there are manufactured devices to hold securely any piece of wood for any possible operation. These new tools, combined with the newer metals for cutting and scraping tools, have gone far towards advancing the creative use of wood on the lathe.

To illustrate the importance of the new devices, let's look at how wood was held in the not too distant past. When I began turning in 1971, there were only a few choices for holding wood for vessel turning. One was the old kraft-paper-and-glue method. This involved making a sandwich of a faceplate screwed to a wooden disc, glue, kraft paper, glue, and the smooth surface of the workpiece. All of this was clamped and dried. After the vessel was turned, it was separated from the sandwich device by inserting a pallet knife between the turning and the kraft paper. The mess of glue and paper was planed or scraped off and the bottom sanded. This method was messy and potentially destructive to the thin edges on the finished turning. For small containers and footed bowls I could have used a 3- or 4-jaw chuck, tightening the wrench until the jaws compressed the wood fibres and gripped the wood. The problem was that the wood was not as hard as the metal, and the chuck grip loosened as the fibres compressed. The jaws would have to be retightened after only a short period. The other method, and my least favorite, was that of screwing wood screws into the end grain of the block of wood. Of course, only a little pressure from the side with a slightly dull tool would have stripped the wood off the screws, causing it to drop or fly off the lathe. A broken window or bruised nose was often the result.

Today some practical solutions are being manufactured for safe use by turners. Nothing revolutionary about these devices, they resemble the ones made by hand turners over the years. But these devices are extremely safe and strong if care is taken in setting them up.

Hot-melt glue. Hot-melt glue is a fast-drying adhesive applied with a gun (Illus. 190). A solid glue stick is melted in the gun as it is pushed through a heated element. The easiest glue gun to use has an advancing trigger to push the glue stick through. The most primitive gun works by advancing the stick with the thumb, an awkward procedure in practice.

The grip of hot-melt glue is very tight, but unlike yellow or white water-based glues, the hot glue barely penetrates the wood surface. The thin bead of glue that bonds the workpiece disc to the faceplate disc (Illus. 191) is brittle and can be easily broken by a slight rap on the turning with a soft mallet or by separating the discs with a pallet knife. The amount of glue applied is not as important as the evenness of clamping pressure. If uneven pressure is applied the mounting will be lopsided. A few lines of glue is all that is needed. Clamp the discs in a workbench vise for a minute or so, and you are ready to turn.

This work-holding method is an updated version of the old kraft-paper-and-glue approach. The hot-melt–glue method is much cleaner, however, and does not cause as much waste after turning is completed. It is useful for making flat-bottomed plates, container

Illus. 190. Hot-melt–glue gun with solid glue stick.

Illus. 191. Hot-melt–glue work-holding method. A thin bead of glue bonds the workpiece disc, left, to the faceplace disc, right.

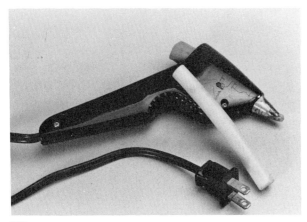

190

191

lids, etc. This process can accommodate fairly large plates and bowls, although anything over 10 in. (25.4 cm) is not practical.

The hot-glue method requires a faceplate, the most basic work-holding device, which is described in detail on pages 172–73. The small 3-in. (76-mm) size is appropriate for most turnings. It is screwed to a parallel-surfaced wooden disc 3 in. (76 mm) or larger in diameter. Although plywood is often used for the disc because it is sold with parallel sides, I prefer to use a piece of pine or oak. It is easier to shape the surface of solid wood than plywood, and I don't like to battle the glue in the plywood to keep an edge on my tool. The face of the disc can be trued with a straight scraper using the technique for flattening bowl interiors or bottoms explained in the techniques section (page 200). Check the surface with a straightedge held across the entire face of the disc. Any light peeking through will indicate inaccuracy.

After the disc is cut and surfaced, the next step is to mark the block. Take a pair of dividers and penetrate the point of one leg into the center point of the turning wood. Of course, the tool rest is brought up near the center line for this and is positioned close to the wood. Stop the lathe, and with the divider point at the center, spread the other leg out to the perimeter of the disc, thus taking a measurement of the radius of the circle. Tighten the divider and transfer this circle to the bottom of the previously cut workpiece disc. The workpiece disc can now be accurately positioned on the approximate center of the faceplate disc by fitting the faceplate disc into the circle drawn on the workpiece disc.

Double-stick tape.   The setup for using the double-stick–tape method is the same as that for the hot-melt–glue method. The same faceplate, wood disc with parallel sides, and center-finding method apply. The double-stick tape is spread over a fair amount of the faceplate disc so that the grip on the workpiece disc will be as strong as possible. The removal method is also the same, and the tape can be peeled off after use. The double-stick–tape method is practical for small or medium-sized, lightweight pieces only.

Screw chuck.   The screw chuck is the simplest method for mounting the wood on the lathe. Most screw chucks have a threaded mounting sleeve that fits over the spindle on the headstock, with a single screw protruding from the center of the sleeve. All screw chucks are not the same.

The earliest type of screw chuck that I had was a Morse taper ring with a simple wood screw tightened into it. This device had two major problems with it. First, the Morse taper was only a press that fitted into the headstock and was prone to come loose (often) while turning. Second, the screw that was used was a wood screw. Wood screws have a very coarse thread and are shaped like an ice cream cone. This is fine for screwing two pieces of wood together but not good for turning. The coarse thick thread left the wood crest between the spirals weak and therefore did not provide a strong enough hold. In addition, the cone-shaped screw did not match up to the cylindrical pilot hole made by the brad-point or twist drill.

The chuck was definitely one that could stand some improvement. The ideal would seem to be a chuck that screwed on tight to the headstock and had a center screw with a knifelike thread shaped overall like a cylinder (Illus. 192). See Illus. 193 for an example of a handmade version of this ideal chuck made in the 1970s by Jake Brubaker. It represents the inspiration for the improved models we see on the market today. The two machine-made models (Glaser and Crafts Supplies USA chucks) in Illus. 193 work so well that it is possible to remove the wood from the chuck and afterwards screw it back again retaining the same tight grip, a procedure that would be unheard of using the earlier screw-chuck design. Both of these screw chucks also have a recessed center with a ridge that surrounds the face of the chuck. This is an excellent idea because it provides a firm grip even if the wooden disc is not perfectly flat. The ridge is only actually touching a small part of the surface of the wood.

The method of mounting the screw chuck to the wood block is very simple. The face of the wood must be reasonably flat and not cupped. A hole must be drilled on the workpiece disc with a drill the size of the pilot section of the screw on the screw chuck (Illus. 194). The drilled hole must be as perpendicular to the surface of the wood as possible.

After the hole is drilled, mount the wood on the chuck. One easy method of doing this is to place the screw chuck on the headstock and engage the indexing mechanism on the headstock. The workpiece disc can then be tightened onto the chuck. Don't forget to disengage the indexing mechanism before turning on the lathe. Oc-

Illus. 192. Ideally shaped and threaded screw for the basic screw chuck.

Illus. 193. Four screw chucks (left to right): Glaser chuck, Brubaker chuck, Crafts Supply USA chuck, and old-style Hegner chuck.

Illus. 194. Workpiece with a hole drilled to the size of the pilot section of the screw chuck.

Illus. 195. A plumber's strap wrench can be very useful in loosening a chuck that has become frozen on the headstock.

casionally the chuck will become frozen on the headstock, and because it is smooth and round, it can be very difficult to remove.

I have grown very fond of a device called a strap wrench (Illus. 195), which was designed for loosening plated plumbing pipes. By making the rubbery strap tight and levering the chuck around a half of a turn, the turner can loosen the chuck in seconds without difficulty. One good way to keep chucks from freezing on the headstock spindle is to make a round washer out of inner tube rubber big enough to fit around the headstock spindle. This will form a buffer between the chuck and the shoulder of the headstock. I use the screw chuck to hold plates and bowls for turning the outside and bottom surfaces.

192   193

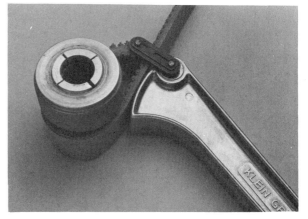

194   195

Faceplate. Faceplate work-holding devices are basic and simple. Like the screw chuck, the faceplate device has a threaded sleeve that fits onto the headstock spindle. A faceplate device lies flat against the flat surface of the wood, and three or more screws are fitted through the back of the faceplate and into the wood block. There are a couple of fine points to these devices that will make them work better.

First, let's look at the types of faceplates that are currently available. One is the simple countersunk hole device (Illus. 196) that provides holes in a number of locations. Some or all of these holes can be used to secure the wood on the faceplate. Another device is the slotted faceplate (Illus. 197), which features variable placement

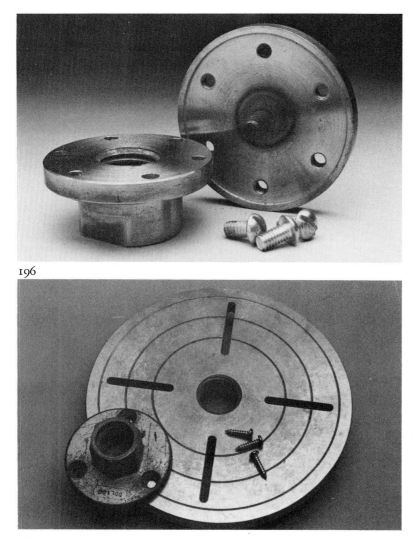

196

197

Illus. 196. The Crafts Supply USA screw chuck doubles as a basic counter-sunk-hole faceplate device.

Illus. 197. A faceplate device that features slots for variable placement of screws.

of the screws along the slots. For relatively small work in which the faceplate is attached to the hollow or waste side of the vessel, the small faceplate with countersunk fixed holes works fine. If however the wood is burly with gaps and hollow spots spread around the piece, use the variable screw placement available in the slotted faceplate. A fixed-hold faceplate can also be drilled with standard high-speed–steel twist drills to incorporate new hole positions, because most faceplates are made of a soft cast material.

It is good maintenance to keep the surface of the faceplate clean of glue or dirt. When acquiring a new faceplate, check to see if the face has been trued or if it is warped. If the faceplate is not too bad you will be able to do any touch-up truing with a high-speed–steel skew scraper. A sharp burr on the edge of the scraper and a straight-edge ruler are all that is needed to cut and check your progress. One good tip for using all faceplates is to use sheet-metal screws instead of wood screws. They grip better, and the head slot is hardened and longer lasting.

Six-in-one chuck. Earlier in this chapter I spoke about the problems I've found with the old-fashioned, 3- or 4-jaw chucks. Their small metal jaws compressed the wood, and their grip actually loosened after only a short time. Until a few years ago, these primitive and inadequate chucks were the only ones available. But about ten years ago a chuck that could hold wood on either the inside (hollow) or the outside diameter of the block was designed by Roy and Peter Child.

This ideal mechanism, called the coil grip chuck, combined a number of holding devices in one body. The primary holding devices included a faceplate, screw chuck, and what is called a ring chuck. The ring chuck was attached to a stepped flange that had to be turned on the end of a square block of wood. This device helped to solve the problem of wood screws stripping out of the end grain of a block while turning—the bane of all beginners. But this chuck was only the start.

Next, Peter Child developed the expanding collet chuck (Illus. 198). Made out of wood, the prototype fit into the coil grip chuck, and the outside ring of the chuck was tightened down, causing the many jaws of the wooden chuck to spread out. The expanding collets fit into an undercut recess with angled sides that matched the angle on the expanding collets gripping the recess around its edge. A very logical and tight way to hold the wood. Different sizes of expanding collets could be made to accommodate different sizes of bowl bottoms.

The expanding collet chuck was later included in a device manufactured with machined steel and aluminum castings known as the six-in-one chuck (Illus. 199). The revolutionary aspects of this device were in the collet and ring chuck functions. The ring chuck is interesting and worth mentioning, although I prefer to use the collet chuck to grip the outside of the block of wood. When, for ex-

198

Illus. 198. The prototype, right, *for the expanding collet chuck,* left, *designed by Peter Child.*

Illus. 199. The six-in-one chuck is manufactured with machined-steel and aluminum castings.

199

ample, turning a goblet, you need to hold the end of the block tightly without support from the tailstock end because that is where the hollow of the goblet goes. Putting screws into the end grain doesn't work for reasons discussed earlier, so it would be best to grip the wood in some way around its perimeter.

One solution is the ring chuck. Its usefulness in certain jobs soon becomes apparent after learning how to assemble it. The block of wood is first mounted between the drive center and the ball-bearing center. Next, a round, stepped flange is turned on one end of the block. The half or third section of the removable ring chuck is used as a template to make the smaller step of the flange, and the diameter at the end of the block represents the larger step of the flange. The flange is passed through the outer ring of the chuck. Around the flange are placed all of the pieces of the removable ring chuck which also fits into the matching hole in the outer ring of the chuck. The entire assembly is then tightened onto the remaining body parts of the chuck until the outer ring cannot be tightened any more, and the wood is held firmly. The parting tool is used to make the flange and is also used to make the final parting cut to remove the turned goblet from the flange held in the chuck. This chuck enables the turner to work on any part of the wood block including the end.

The expanding collet device is the real advantage of the six-in-one chuck. The kraft-paper-and-glue, faceplate-and-screws, and other methods require either some cleanup or filling of screw holes after turning and obviously were not perfect for fine pieces of turning. The expanding collet on the other hand fulfilled two purposes. The recess made to hold the chuck could be used as a decorative element of the turning while holding the wood firmly, and it provided less of a bearing surface at the bottom of the piece where it contacted the table top. This last point was important because all wood expands and contracts. The possibility that a bowl might eventually become wobbly was minimized by this thinner rim. The simple concept of the expanding collet is the dovetailed grip that the bevel on the collet sections exert on the matching recess cut into the wood.

Use of the chuck requires a number of steps that are integrated into the vessel-turning process. Initially, the wood is mounted on a faceplate or a screw chuck and the outside of the bowl shape is turned, the bottom of the vessel faced off or flattened, and the dovetailed recess cut. This is the best time to rough, refine cut, and sand the outside shape because it is easier to work on this surface before the hollowing process has removed waste wood. After this wood is removed, stresses are relieved, and the form tends to go out of round, making it more difficult to work. When the desired outside shape has been achieved and the size of the base has been determined, it is necessary to face off the bottom and make the dovetailed recess in it. The bottom can be flattened with the straight scraper, and the recess can be undercut with the skew scraper.

The first step to flattening or facing off the bottom of a plate or bowl is to place the straight tool rest close to the surface of the wood. The uneven surface can be flattened with a bowl gouge, straight scraper, or with a roundnose scraper. With either of the scrapers, the tool is literally pushed straight into the wood and drawn laterally across the surface. Light cuts are best at the start because they are more controllable. My preference is to use the bowl gouge for this operation because the cut is much quicker and because a straight cut is easily accomplished by rubbing the entire bevel along during the cut.

To begin the cut with the gouge I enter the wood with the right side of the cutting edge near the mid-line of the piece (Illus. 200). The tool handle is held low, and the blade is held high. The edge of the bevel is then allowed to penetrate the wood to the depth of cut required to flatten the still rough surface. After this penetration is accomplished with the bevel rubbing the wood, adjust the depth of cut to make a flat surface. Arc the tool towards the center of the piece as shown in Illus. 200b–d.

To make the recess correspond in size with the diameter of the collet chuck, you must mark the bottom using a pair of dividers and a ruler (Illus. 201). If the diameter of the collet chuck is 2½ in. (64 mm), the radius of the dividers should be set at around 1⅛ in. (28 mm). The diameter dimension, when measured with all of the collets bunched together, does not reflect their size when they are expanded in the body of the chuck. This size will be greater, and some allowance must be made for it when making a finishing cut within the recess. With the dividers set at 1⅛ in. (28 mm), position the tool rest across the face of the bottom of the bowl and a little lower than the center of it. Using one leg of the dividers as the center and touching it to the center of the wood, press the other leg into the wood to mark the diameter. This is all done with the lathe

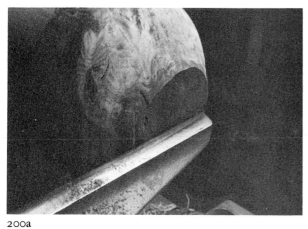

200a

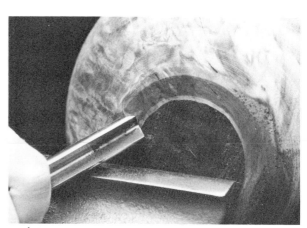

200b

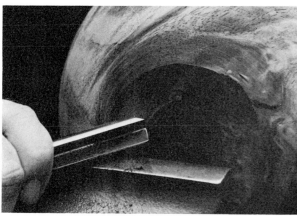

200c

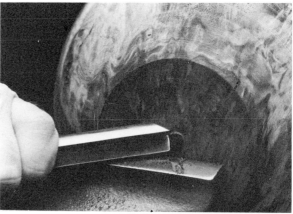

200d

Illus. 200a–d. Flattening the bottom of a bowl with the bowl gouge. From the midline of the piece, the gouge is arced towards the center of the piece.

Illus. 201. With the lathe turned on, mark the bottom recess for the expanding collet chuck using a pair of dividers.

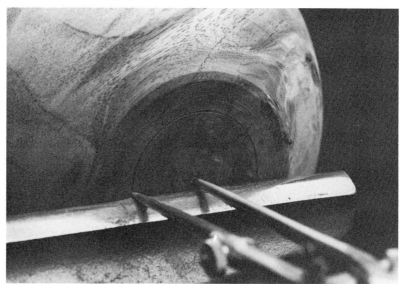

201

turned on. The result is a mark that is used as a starting point for the cutting of the recess. The recess can be hollowed out with the same tools that are used for facing off. Usually the recess is too small for the bowl gouge to be effective. The large skew chisel may also be too large unless the larger 3½-in. (89-mm) expanding collets are going to be used. I prefer to hollow out the rough recess with a small roundnose scraper and to flatten this rough opening with a ½-in. (13-mm) skew chisel (Illus. 202).

To make the cut with the roundnose I push the tool into the wood at any point within the confines of the marked recess. With the blade held horizontal I move the tool laterally with as much control as possible to make the surface I am cutting as flat as possible. After this is done I cut off the tops of the ridges with the edge of the skew chisel held in the same horizontal position as the round-nose scraper. I move the skew chisel laterally and flatten the surface, finishing off with the long point of the chisel forming the undercut perimeter. The recess must be at least ⅛ in. (3 mm) deep to hold the expanding collets firmly. After forming the entire recess, sand it completely with a piece of hand-held sandpaper. After the recess has been hollowed, flattened, undercut, and sanded, it is time to test-fit the expanding collets into it (Illus. 203).

The loosened collets must fit into the recess easily so that there is some room to tighten them. With the wood mounted on the chuck, remove the workpiece from the other chuck, turn it around, and mount the expanding collet chuck on the lathe, using the indexing mechanism again to tighten the outer ring of the chuck as firmly as possible in the wood. One important tip to remember is to make the wall surrounding the recess for this chuck thick and deep enough to withstand the pressure of the chuck while turning. Some woods like mahogany, with their soft brittle grains, are not strong enough to stand the pressure and will splinter out and loosen.

Collet chuck. Called simply the collet chuck, this companion to the expanding collet chuck works in the same way as the ring chuck to grip a round cylinder of wood. As the collet chuck's outside ring is tightened, the collets contract around the perimeter of a round piece of wood, gripping it firmly. To use this device a tenon or smaller cylinder must be turned on one end of the workpiece to match the inside diameter of the collet you plan to use. See the techniques described in chapter 5 (pages 128–33) for using either calipers and a

Illus. 202a,b. Hollow out the rough recess with the roundnose scraper and flatten with the skew chisel.

Illus. 203. Test-fit the expanding collet chuck into the recess.

202a

202b

203

parting tool or a beading tool inserted into the woodturner's sizing tool to cut the tenon. The shoulder of the workpiece at the end of the tenon must be flat and perpendicular for strong support because it presses against the face of the collet chuck. This type of chuck is perfect for making small finials or other small items because it provides access to all parts including the end for cutting and sanding.

Last word on chucks. The chucks just explained are not the only chucks available. Rather they comprise my basic group of work-holding devices. With them I am prepared to hold any piece of wood for any operation suited to a standard heavy-duty lathe. They are not inexpensive. Screw chucks cost between $30 and $70, and six-in-one chucks can cost over $100. If you plan to make a plate or two this year, it will probably be worthwhile to use the hot-glue or faceplate method.

Marking and Cutting the Disc

Here are some basic steps for marking and cutting out wood for all vessel-mounting approaches. The first step is to mark out the round workpiece disc (Illus. 204) with the pencil compass. If following a plan, make two circles; one will identify the final diameter for the piece and the other the diameter of the faceplate or faceplate disc that will hold the workpiece. Before cutting select the best part of the wood for the piece; avoid holes, cracks, and other flaws. The center point should be made deep enough so that it will be easy to find

Illus. 204. Bowl disc, cut and ready for marking.

again. I put a small circle around the center mark for this purpose. It is also helpful to use colored pencils when working on dark-colored woods such as walnut and rosewood. Yellow pencils work best for me. After the disc has been marked, it is ready to be sawed. If using a band saw, be sure to work on the waste side of the line; it is easy to cut away too much. A precise round is not necessary because the turning cuts on the lathe will make the shape round. Be sure to use the right size blade when cutting the radius. The Appendix at the end of the book lists band saw widths and their corresponding radii.

Occasionally I have used the lathe rather than a saw to cut out the round disc. The sawing procedure is not a long one and certainly worth doing, but the rounding may have to be done on the lathe for some other reason. To do this mount the wood on the work-holding device you plan to use and set the tool rest a little below center across the face of the square. Be sure to check whether the square is touching at any point on the tool rest. Use a parting tool as you would for spindle work and cut out the round shape on the outside of the drawn line. As you get close to the bottom of the cut, the sound will get higher in pitch. This would be a good time to stop and break off the outer waste from the disc to eliminate potential tearing or chipping.

Mounting the Block

After the workpiece block has been drilled for the faceplate or screw chuck or preturned for the expanding collet chuck or contracting collet chuck, it must be mounted on the lathe. Always test the tightness of the chuck in the wood a couple of times so there will be no surprises later on (Illus. 205). Position the tool-rest base and the tool rest as close as possible to the wood block without touching it. Then revolve the wood by hand to check for any obstructions (Illus. 206). If the wood is eccentric or has a number of bumps such as those found on a burl, position the tailstock so that it will support the block until it is more round and balanced. Determining the appropriate motor speed for the size of the block is easy with a variable-speed pulley on the motor. Simply dial the speed lever as high as it will go without causing too much vibration. For nonvariable speed of fixed pulleys, estimate the appropriate speed and set the belt on those pulleys. Then turn on the machine and wait for the block to revolve a bit while keeping your hand on the switch in case

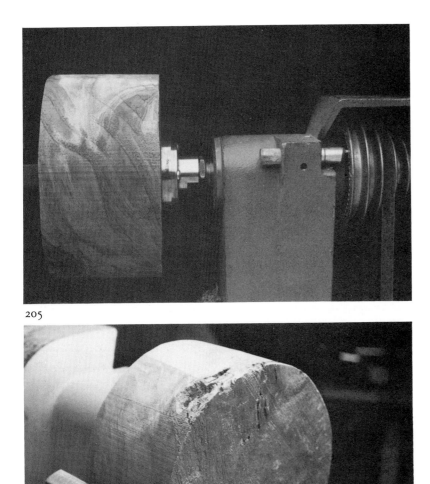

205

206

Illus. 205. Bowl disc mounted on the screw chuck in the headstock.

Illus. 206. Position the tool rest close to the wooden disc and check for obstructions by hand rotating the disc prior to turning on the lathe.

the vibration is too great and the speed must be lowered. A table of speeds and corresponding wood sizes is included in the Appendix.

Safety

The safety measures for vessel turning are the same as those for spindle turning. Always be aware of the gap that exists between the tool rest and the wood and never allow any loose clothing, hair, or even steel wool to get caught on a revolving piece of wood. There are a number of situations that may occur while turning a vessel, and knowledge of them, the havoc they can wreak, and how to avoid them will help to eliminate the initial fear of working on the lathe.

If the block of wood is not mounted securely on a screw chuck or faceplate it will wobble while turning and any pressure against it with a turning tool will exacerbate the problem. If the screws are loose, the block may make contact with the tool rest and cause a rattle. The same action is evident if the collets become loose. If the block of wood is loose and no tool is touching it, the wood will usually spin off the mount and bounce away from you. If pressure is applied to the block with a tool, it might spin erratically, fly off, and hit you. With modern chucks this is not likely, but listen for the first sign of a suspicious noise and stop the lathe immediately. Lock the indexing mechanism in the headstock and check the tightness of the wood on the chuck.

Another possible way to stop inadvertently the rotation of the wood and loosen a chuck's hold is to position the tool rest too close to the wood. One of the bumps can therefore make contact with the tool rest. If the belt is not tight on the pulleys it will slip, and no torque will be put on the drive pulley. Turn off the motor as soon as possible and readjust the rest. Don't try to adjust the rest with the motor on; this could make the situation even worse. A deeper than usual cut with the turning tool in green wood can stop the rotation but it will usually continue after pulling the tool from the wood. Sometimes rotation stops because the motor does not have enough power or the belts are too loose on the pulleys. Check the belt first. Motors smaller than 1 h.p. will always make turning large bowls frustrating. The power is simply inadequate to push the wood through the cut.

The Rounded Shape

The first step in vessel turning is to form the outside rounded shape. This operation is first because it is always more difficult to work on the outside after all of the wood is removed from the hollow or inside of the vessel. As mentioned in an earlier section, relieving the wood's natural stress by removing the mass of the waste wood leaves the turned, thin wall very flexible. Centrifugal force combined with the pressure from the tool makes controlled cutting on the outside of a hollow vessel very difficult.

Bowl gouge. Roughing cuts render the sawed disc round and remove all of the bumps, edges, and saw marks. In truth any gouge can be used to do this, but the most appropriate is a bowl gouge. The bowl gouge combines the deep roughing shape and moderate width necessary to remove wood quickly and still minimize tear-out and chipping. After determining the appropriate motor speed, position the tool rest close to the wood, lower than the middle, and place the tool blade on top of the rest with the handle held low. The blade must be perpendicular to the surface of the block, and the center of the bottom of the blade must be on the rest.

To begin the cut, rub the bevel on the wood lightly. It will bump a little but that's acceptable. Lift the handle gently until the edge begins to cut (Illus. 207). It is the position of the handle that determines the depth of cut, and in the beginning make several passes removing only the tops of the bumps. After testing for the appropriate depth of cut, slide the blade back and forth along the tool rest until the block is cylindrical. With good lighting, shadows will appear on top of the block, caused by the eccentricities of the rough wood gradually being eliminated.

After the round disc is made, a more refined shaping of the form can begin. It is now possible to remove more wood on each pass because the wood is smooth. A bowl gouge can also be used for shaping because it leaves a relatively smooth surface. For the shaping cut again rub the bevel with the handle low, but this time rock the blade onto its side and use the lower side of the cutting edge (Illus. 208).

Illus. 207a–c. Sequence of roughing cuts to make the disc smooth for the shaping operation.

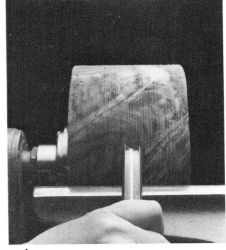

207a   207b   207c

This part of the edge is firmly supported on the tool rest. The inside or hollow of the gouge is facing in the direction of the cut. It is important to remember the basic rule of turning—always proceed from a larger diameter to a smaller diameter (Illus. 209) and never attempt to cut on a return stroke. With the bevel rubbing on the wood behind the cut and the lower part of the cutting edge firmly supported on the tool rest, the cut is clean and quick. The constantly rubbing bevel produces a lot of friction and heat, which can burn the hand on the tool rest as it is drawn up the blade. Some turners wear a leather glove for protection.

After forming the basic shape, it is a good idea to make a final finishing cut to eliminate some of the ridges left by the roughing and shaping cuts. For this cut, the shallow side of the bowl-gouge edge is used (Illus. 210). The handle is again low and the tool is rolled over to the edge opposite to the one used for shaping. Push this shallow edge along the surface, making sure the corner doesn't dig in. If the corner does dig in, it will be unsupported on the tool rest and will cause a tear-out in the wood as it is slammed down onto the rest.

Illus. 208a,b. Rock the bowl gouge blade onto its side and use the lower side of the cutting edge to make basic shaping cuts.

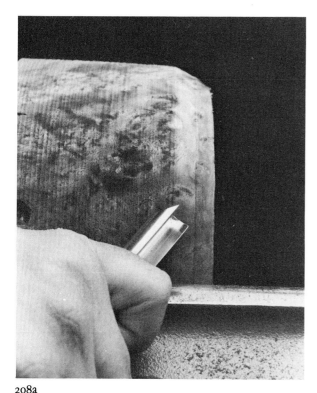

208a

208b

209a

209b

Illus. 209a,b. Proceeding from the larger to the smaller diameter, hold the handle low and slowly raise it to a nearly horizontal position to end the shaping cut.

Illus. 210. To eliminate ridges left by roughing and shaping cuts, make finishing cuts with the shallow side of the bowl gouge.

210

Finesse is necessary to make a smooth, controlled cut that will result in a smooth surface. These roughing, shaping, and smoothing cuts are made the same way with either the Superflute or the Stocksdale bowl gouges.

Steps for roughing with the bowl gouge:
- ☐ Position the tool rest close to the work and below the center of the wood.
- ☐ With the handle low, position the tool with the bottom center of the blade on the tool rest.
- ☐ Allow the bevel to lightly rub the revolving wood. Keep the blade perpendicular to the surface of the wood.
- ☐ Lift the handle lightly until small shavings are cut off.
- ☐ Slide the blade along the tool rest from side to side until the disc is round.

Steps for shaping with the bowl gouge:
- ☐ Position the rest close to the work and below the center of the wood.
- ☐ With the handle low and the blade on its side facing in the direction of the cut, place the blade on the tool rest.
- ☐ Allow the bevel to rub the wood, while adjusting the handle for the appropriate depth of cut.
- ☐ Move the handle towards you and away from the perpendicular.
- ☐ Proceed through the cut, with the bevel rubbing and the bottom part of the edge cutting the shape.

Steps for finishing the shape with the bowl gouge:
- ☐ Position the tool rest close to the work and below the center of the wood.
- ☐ With the handle low and the blade rotated so that the blade channel is facing away from the cut, use the edge opposite to the one used for roughing and shaping and push through the wood with a smooth motion and good control.

Roundnose scraper. The roundnose scraper is an inappropriate tool for rounding over, but it is sometimes used for shallow hollowing in conjunction with the rounding-over process on the outside of a vessel (Illus. 211).

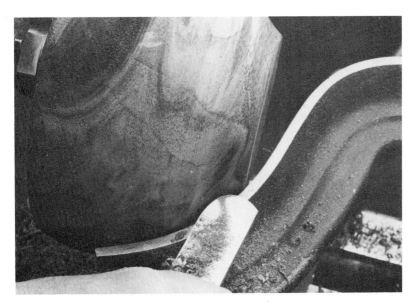

Illus. 211. The roundnose scraper is sometimes used for shallow hollowing on the outside of a vessel.

To use the roundnose scraper for roughing out a hollow section, choose a size appropriate to the size of the depression that you wish to make. Bring the tool rest up close to the wood and locate it high enough so that the cutting edge of the scraper is horizontal with the center of the turning. Now the depth of cut can be adjusted without having the handle in an awkward position. It is the burr on the end of the blade that does the cutting, so begin again by rubbing a small portion of the bevel on the wood with the blade in a horizontal position. Lift the handle slightly while pressing lightly into the revolving wood. The sharp burr combined with the proper angle will produce the shavings typical of any cutting tool. If only powder is produced, adjust the handle angle by lifting up slightly. If this still does not produce shavings, regrind the burr. A smooth, even stroke as the blade glides along the smooth tool rest will produce fair, rounded curves.

Steps for shallow hollowing with the roundnose scraper:
- ☐ Position the tool rest close to the wood but with a gap of about ¼ to ⅜ in. (6 to 10 mm) between the tool rest and the surface of the wood.
- ☐ Position the tool rest high enough so that the cutting edge of the tool is horizontal with the center line of the wood.
- ☐ With the handle approximately in the horizontal position, lift

slightly until the burr begins cutting, and fine shavings are produced.

□ Glide the blade along the tool rest to produce an even, rounded shape.

Skew and square-ended scrapers. An alternative to the bowl gouge for rounding over a surface is the square-ended scraper. The straight edge can be pivoted on the tool rest to make light, glancing cuts that round over shapes (Illus. 212). A more precise cut is possible with a scraper than with a gouge (Illus. 213). Precision is sometimes necessary to conform to dimensions on a blueprint. The scraper cuts much slower than a gouge, and the quality of the cut is inferior to the smooth shaved surface produced by a gouge cut. I like to use my skew scraper for shaping and have ground a bevel on the long pointed side for 1 in. (25 mm) or so of its length. The added side bevel turns the tool into a side cutter useful for enlarging drilled holes and for rounding over the lip of a bowl. I use the straight end of the cutting edge for flattening. The techniques for using the skew and square-ended scrapers are the same as those described above for using the roundnose scraper.

The Hollow Shape

My approach to making a hollow vessel takes advantage of the current work-holding technology. First, I shape the outside and the

Illus. 212. To round over a surface, use the square-ended scraper as an alternative to the bowl gouge.

213a

213b

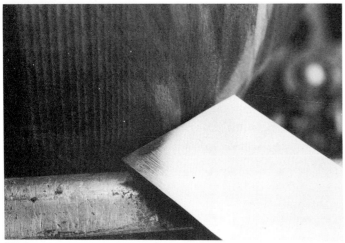

213c

Illus. 213a–c. Sequence in detail of rounding over with a square-ended scraper.

bottom of the workpiece, as outlined on pages 183–89. Next, I reverse the workpiece on the lathe by attaching one of the mounting devices to the finished bottom. Then I remove the wood from the inside, creating a hollow. This approach enables me to work over the bed of the lathe for as much of the turning process as possible. It is very difficult to work on the outside of the bowl form in any other way because of the limitations of the lathe bed, the tool rest, and the tool-rest base. They simply can't accommodate and support finish and detail turning on the bottom. It is for this reason that many turners use the outboard end of the headstock for hollow-vessel turning. In addition, I prefer the finished look of a clean, flat bottom or with a cleanly cut recess made for a work-holding chuck. It takes a little more time, but in the context of a well-turned piece it enhances the final product. This process works well for turning dry and burl wood. For green wood some modification must be made to account for the wood movement that occurs while the piece is drying. These are illustrated on pages 229–39 in the chapter on wood.

The first step in hollowing out is to drill a depth-locating hole. I use a multispur machine bit with a piece of black tape wrapped around that part of the drill shank that corresponds to the depth desired in the block (Illus. 214). This is not the finished depth, however. In fact, it can be as much as $\frac{3}{16}$ in. (4.5 mm) short of the finished bottom of the hollow because the center point of the drill and additional refining of the shape must be taken into account. The depth hole also makes cutting easier. Working from the central area near the hole it functions as the central relief for the cuts, and there is no knob or hill in the center of the turning to be removed.

The bowl gouge is the first tool used to remove waste wood in the hollow of the bowl. This tool is followed by scrapers, which continue the hollowing and also refine the cut shape with light cuts of their own.

Bowl gouge. In many ways the methods used to rough out and shape the outside of the bowl form are repeated on the inside of the form but in reverse. The bowl gouge is used exclusively to remove the bulk of the waste from the inside of the hollow. It is well suited to this task because it has a deep enough hollow in the center of the blade to take a deep cut without the blade corners becoming buried in the wood. The bowl gouge is long and provides the added lever-

214a

214b

Illus. 214a,b. Before starting the hollowing operation, drill a depth-locating hole with a multispur bit.

age needed to maintain control of the tool while cutting deep inside the bowl form. When preparing to use the bowl gouge, first consider the position of the tool rest. It is more important for the tool rest to be located close to the surface of the wood in the hollowing operation than in rounding over, because it is easy to catch the edge of the tool in the wood when making a concave shape. The special bowl-turning rest has curves to match those on the emerging hollow

(Illus. 215), and with it we can get as close as we need for the best control.

To begin cutting, remove the corner near the depth hole (Illus. 216). As in all cutting operations, work from the large diameter to the small diameter, in this case towards the center. The blade rests on its side with the center channel of the blade facing away from the center of the hollow. Only the lower curve of the blade edge must be allowed to touch the wood, and therefore the handle must be held low. A bit of adjustment will always be necessary to get the tool to cut properly in this position, and such adjustment is always done on the handle end of the tool. With the bevel rubbing against the wood, start the cut. This is the safest way to start because the bevel supports the tool blade on the surface of the wood and continues to lend stability in the freshly cut wood throughout the manœuvre.

The most difficult part of this cut is the initial penetration. The edge of the blade must be held high on the tool rest, and the handle must be twisted slightly to put the lower part of the edge in contact with the wood. An intermediate step can be of help both in the mastery of this cutting technique and in the successful completion of the hollowing process prior to mastery. It consists of cutting a series of concentric ridges or fences, which measure ⅛ to 3/16 in. (3 to 4.5 mm) in depth, into the face of the block with a skew chisel held

Illus. 215. Bowl-turning tool rests with curves to match a bowl's hollow shape enhance tool control.

horizontally on the tool rest. These fences become the starting points for each succeeding cut and give firm support to the bevel from the very start of each cut. By placing the bevel in against the fence and adjusting the handle in a low position to begin the cut you will be able to develop the sensitivity necessary to control depth of cut (Illus. 217).

After the penetration of the wood, the next important consideration is the motion made by the tool in following through and completing the cut. The edge of the tool is positioned fairly high on the tool rest in the beginning of the cut, and it must arc down into the center of the blank to do the best cutting (Illus. 218). If the edge is started low on the tool rest, or actually in a horizontal position, too

Illus. 216a–d. To begin the hollowing operation, remove the corner near the depth hole.

216a

216b

216c

216d

Illus. 217. With the skew chisel, make a series of concentric fences. These will serve as starting points for succeeding cuts made by the bowl gouge in the intermediate stage of the hollowing operation.

little of the cutting edge will be in contact with the wood and the work will go too slowly. While the edge arcs in towards the center of the block, the handle follows along and is raised in a smooth motion that raises the handle end progressively higher. The handle will be nearly horizontal at the end of the cut. Resist the temptation to cut on the backstroke. This consititutes working uphill or from the smaller to the larger diameter; the tool is insecurely supported, and it is very easy to catch the opposite part of the cutting edge in the wood. The result of this type of catch will be a tear-out.

As with all cutting tools, the handle controls the depth of cut with the bevel acting as a fulcrum. If you take too deep a cut and need a way to get out of the resulting rut, stop the cut but leave the tool in with the bevel rubbing lightly (Illus. 219). Make a slight adjustment by moving the handle towards you a little and use the heel of the bevel edge as a fulcrum. Every slight movement towards the body reduces the depth of cut. A couple of these shallower passes will eliminate the rut initially created.

After the basic hollow form has been roughed out, it will be difficult to continue with the gouge, unless the hollow of the bowl is to be shaped like a cone (Illus. 220). But the bowl gouge has some limitations when the hollow is to be deep and more cylindrical. When this point is reached, it is time to turn to the roundnose roughing scraper to remove the remaining waste prior to refining the shape.

218a

218b

218c

218d

218e

Illus. 218a–e. This sequence shows the motion of the gouge as it is arced from a fairly high position down into the center of the blank.

Illus. 219a,b. To get out of a rut created by cutting too deeply, use the heel of the bevel as a fulcrum by moving the handle towards you slightly and taking shallow cuts until the rut is removed.

Illus. 220. The bowl gouge will eventually produce a cone shape. Replace it with the roundnose scraper to remove the remaining waste and widen the bowl bottom.

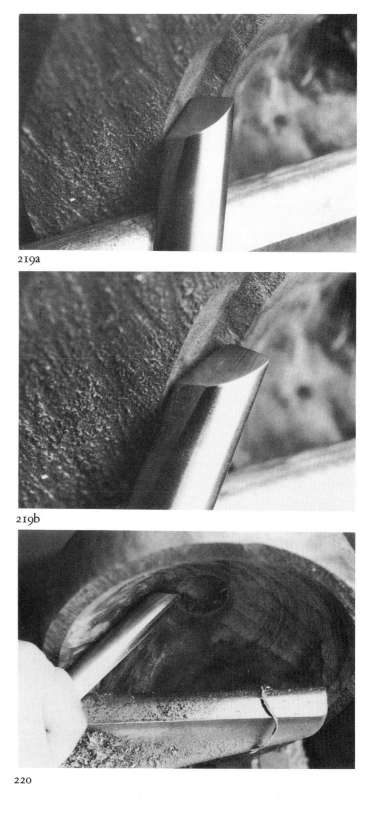

219a

219b

220

After shaping outside and bottom of the workpiece as outlined on pages 183–89, follow these steps for hollowing with the bowl gouge:

☐ Reverse vessel and attach mounting device to finished bottom.
☐ Drill a depth-locating hole with multispur machine bit.
☐ Place the tool rest close to the face of the block.
☐ Begin the cut with the tool handle held low and the inside channel of the blade facing away from the center of the wood and placed on its side on the rest.
☐ Begin hollowing near the central depth hole.
☐ Make the hollowing cut with the lower edge of the blade by arcing towards the center of the wood while raising the handle from a low position to a horizontal one in one fluid sweep.

Roundnose scraper. After all of the cutting has been completed with the bowl gouge and the vessel is roughly hollowed out, the final refining cuts must be made prior to sanding. The tool used for this is the roundnose scraper. The roughing out with the bowl gouge leaves a series of concentric ridges if the work is done quickly, or a reasonable smooth surface with broad bumps if a final finishing cut is made to remove those ridges. The precise control possible with the roundnose scraper is needed to produce fair, even curves and to refine the surface. It is possible to buy massive scrapers, ⅜ in. (10 mm) thick, with broad cutting edges to produce this fair shape. I prefer a lighter tool because it is easier to make the smooth fluid stroke that will produce the smooth fluid surface. For this technique, I use a 1¼-in. (32-mm) roundnose scraper, which I regrind on the left side of the blade into a long and broad shallow curve. By drawing this edge along the inside surface from the center to the outside edge of the piece in a controlled even motion, I gradually reduce the high spots, thereby consolidating the surface (Illus. 221). This of course goes against the basic rule of working from the larger to the smaller diameter, but there is no danger of a tear-out with the scraping tool because there are no corners to catch in the large diameter of the turning wood.

Steps for using the roundnose scraper for finish cuts after hollowing cuts:

□ Place the rounded, bowl-turning tool rest close to the hollow shape of the inside of the vessel (Illus. 222).

□ Position the tool rest high enough so that the cutting edge of the tool is horizontal with the center line of the workpiece.

□ With the handle approximately in the horizontal position, lift slightly until the burr at the end of the tool begins to cut near the bottom of the hollow.

□ Pull the tool along the rest from the center to the edge of the workpiece in a sweep that approximates the final shape of the curve you are making.

□ Continue to make these cuts, checking frequently with the lathe turned off to see that the bumps and ridges are completely removed.

221

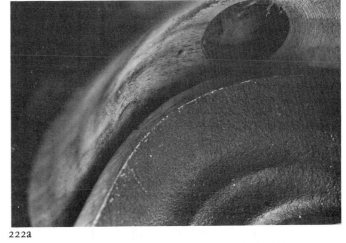

222a

222b

Illus. 221. Rounded bowl-turning tool rest.

Illus. 222a,b. Place the rounded bowl-turning tool rest close to the inside of the vessel and draw the roundnose scraper along the inside surface from the center to the outside edge in a controlled, even motion.

Square-ended scraper. It is often necessary for functional or aesthetic reasons to flatten the interior bottom of a hollow plate or bowl. Flattening this surface is frustrating if attempted with a roundnose scraper or a gouge. There is a straightforward flattening procedure that combines the square-ended scraper and the rotation of the lathe to make an accurate flat surface. Before beginning it is important to check the straightness of the edge of the scraper itself, feeling the burr ground on the edge. If the burr does not feel even along the entire edge, regrind it. Position the tool rest so that the top edge is lower than the center point. The difference between the center point of the turning and the top of the tool rest must, as with all scrapers, be equal to the thickness of the blade of the scraper.

With the wood revolving and the blade held horizontally to the workpiece, position the center of the blade edge at the center point of the turning, the left side of the edge on the left side of the center and the right side of the edge on the right side of the center (Illus. 223). The left edge of the blade should engage and cut the wood, while the right edge should only rub the wood. If these two halves are in contact with the wood at the same time—one cutting, one rubbing—the surface will be flat. Use the flat surface created in the center as the starting point. Step out to the left with incremental cuts to widen this flat area. Finish off by using the roundnose scraper to join the flat area with the rounded sides of the hollow.

Steps for using the square-ended scraper to flatten interior bottom:
- ☐ Position tool rest so that top edge is lower than center point.
- ☐ Hold blade horizontal to workpiece.
- ☐ Position center of blade edge at center point of turning. Left edge should cut wood; right edge should rub only.
- ☐ Make incremental cuts to widen resulting flat area.
- ☐ Use roundnose scraper to join flat bottom and rounded sides.

The skew scraper with the added side bevel is helpful for rounding over bowl and plate edges. The top surface can be rounded or flattened by pivoting the end of the skew scraper on the tool rest while cutting (Illus. 224). The scraper is held horizontally for this operation so that the cutting edge will contact the wood. For making sweeping cuts to finish off or round over the inside of the lip of a bowl, the best edge to use is the bevelled side cutting edge (Illus. 225). The pivoting motion is very slight and the tool is drawn out of the bowl towards you to make the cut.

Illus. 223. To flatten the inside hollow of a bowl or plate with a square-ended scraper, place the center of the blade edge at the center of the turning. (a) The left side of the edge should engage the wood while the right side of the edge should only rub the wood. (b and c) Step out to the left with incremental cuts to widen the flat area in the center.

Illus. 224. To flatten or round over the bowl edge, pivot the end of the skew scraper on the tool rest.

Illus. 225. The bevelled side cutting edge of the skew scraper is used to make sweeping cuts drawn out of the bowl to finish off or round over the inside lip of a bowl.

223a

223b

223c

224

225

Illus. 226. Ideally, the spindle should be sanded end to end, following the direction of the grain.

VII · Sanding and Finishing

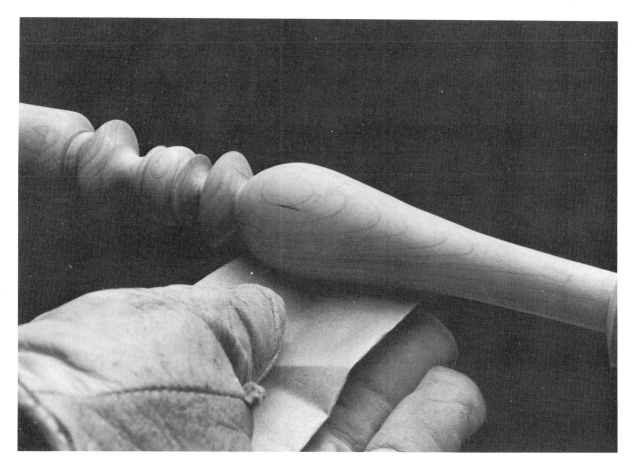

*T*he secret to smooth surfaces is in making smooth finishing cuts after the shape has been roughed out. With practice there is no reason to have to sand any part of a spindle. Vessels can be sanded easily with a power sander. Whenever sanding is required, however, be sure it is done well, for no amount of lacquer or shellac will disguise a poorly sanded surface.

Sanding

Sanding is the most tedious and loathsome of all turning activities. Turners will do anything to reduce the amount of sanding required to finish a piece. Good tool work with sharp tools is one step towards reducing the amount of sanding. The other is to use power sanders whenever possible. Spindles are a particular problem because sanding on a highly decorated spindle must be across the grain. If a coarse grade such as an 80-grit is used at the start of the sanding, we must proceed through a series of finer grits to eliminate torn fibres and scratches left by each preceding grade. Unfortunately, this process alters the shape of details or rounds over a sharp edge. The best way to sand a spindle is end to end, following the direction of the grain (Illus. 226). However, the only time that this is practical is on long hollows, tapers, or cylinders.

Sanding is necessary only if there are hills created by erratic tool work that must be reduced. On hollows this is done best by wrapping sandpaper around a piece of dowel and rolling the dowel in the cove or hollow with the lathe on (Illus. 227). The firm backing of the dowel makes the sanding easier, and your hand will not be subjected to the heat generated. You must keep the sandpaper moving at all times because resting the paper too long in any one place can create deep ridges that will have to be sanded out. The best approach to sanding inside of sharp details is with abrasive-coated cords (Illus. 228) or with cloth strips in varying diameters and widths.

Most sandpaper will quickly accumulate sanding dust at the high speeds necessary to revolve the wood. Move quickly along the paper, always using a fresh cutting surface. A dull section of abrasive paper on which the sharp points of the abrasive have worn off will create more heat than dust and can leave a black or brown ring on the surface of the wood. This will then take even more abrasive to remove. For most sanding, I use the least expensive garnet paper sheets. Heavier weights are a waste of money because the abrasive doesn't last long enough to make full use of its durability. The more expensive bluish white No-fil papers sold in auto body shops are the fastest cutting and longest lasting of all the papers I have used. These types of sandpapers are particularly useful for sanding cured varnish finishes, which tend to accumulate quickly on the paper.

The nemesis for sanding turned bowls is called end-grain patch. Turning of plates and bowls exposes end grain and edge grain on both the inside and the outside of the round and hollow form. This means that both the inside and outside will have two end-grain

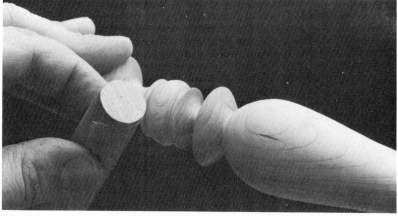

227

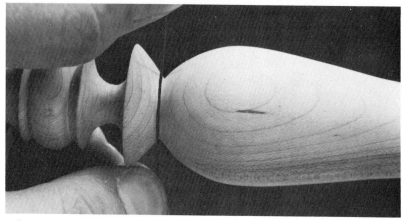

228

Illus. 227. To sand the spindle hollows, wrap sandpaper around a piece of dowel and roll the dowel in the hollow with the lathe turned on.

Illus. 228. Sand inside spindle details with abrasive-coated cloth cords or strips, which are available in various diameters and widths.

patches to remove. Extremely careful scraping with a freshly sharpened tool can eliminate much of the end-grain fuzziness. But most must be removed by sanding.

Recently I have been able to eliminate most of the sanding, sometimes as much as 90%, by using a drill-mounted, soft-rubber–backed disc sanding attachment (Illus. 229) for my power drill. After satisfactory cutting and scraping of the inside and outside surfaces, I turn on the lathe and press the pad of the spinning disc against the wood. Only one third to one half of the disc's surface will be in contact with the wood at any time. The safest position for the pad is on the lower half of the workpiece. The pad's broad surface bridges gaps and ridges and also rounds the surface evenly. After the wood has been evenly covered with fine, swirling scratches (Illus. 230) with the lathe turning counterclockwise, reverse the rotation to clockwise and abrade the fibres that were flattened. It is normal for the end-grain fibres that stick up to lean a little in one direction after being cut. They can be felt by rubbing your hand against the wood in the opposite direction with the lathe stopped. These end-grain patches are also visible as dull sections against the shinier, sanded areas surrounding it.

On my lathe I can reverse the rotation of the workpiece by engaging the handle on the reversing switch. Using the reversing switch, as mentioned earlier, is an inexpensive solution. If you don't have a reversing switch, remove the V-belt from one of the pulleys, twist it

Illus. 229. Rubber-backed disc sanding attachment for a power drill.

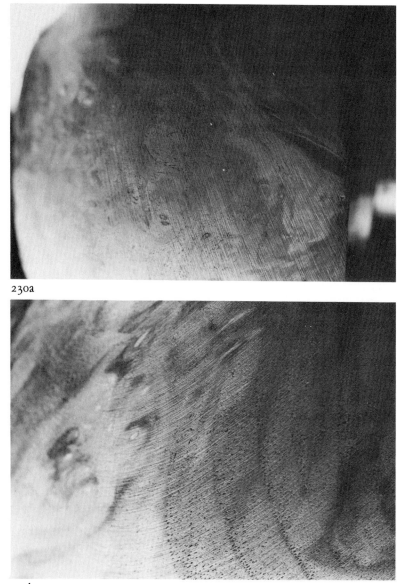

230a

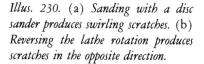

230b

Illus. 230. (a) Sanding with a disc sander produces swirling scratches. (b) Reversing the lathe rotation produces scratches in the opposite direction.

into a figure eight, and reinstall it on the pulley. This will change the direction of rotation with only minor inconvenience.

Disc sanding in this reversed direction will eliminate most of the swirl marks on the surface. The safest position for the disc sander in reversed rotation is either on the opposite side of the lathe with the disc held on the lower half of the workpiece, or on the usual side of the lathe with the disc held on the upper half of the work (Illus. 231).

Illus. 231. When reversing the lathe rotation, place the disc sander on the upper half of the workpiece for optimum safety.

After the wood has been covered with small sanding scratches in both directions, complete the sanding by hand with 220- or 280-grit paper. It is best to back up sandpaper with a felt pad when sanding inside the hollow or with a felt pad or cork block when sanding the rounded outside. For sanding smaller hollows and rounds, pads and blocks are awkward, and it might be easier to back up the paper by wearing a leather glove (Illus. 232). Hand sanding will take very little time if the disc sanding was done carefully. If, after a small amount of hand sanding, small end-grain patches appear, do more disc sanding in the area of the blemish alone.

After using the sandpaper, use steel wool to make even finer scratches. Again, success with the steel wool will depend on the quality of the sanding that went before it. I rarely have to use steel wool any coarser than 4/0 (or 0000) for this operation. I always take a new pad of steel wool and unroll it. After it is unrolled into a long strip I roll it up into a loose pad. This way much more of the possible sanding surface can be used. With the lathe on, move the ball of wool quickly from side to side across the wood. Steel-wool sanding will produce a soft, even sheen. With the lathe stopped, run a hand along the surface of the wood and small pieces of steel wool can be felt in the fibres of the wood. This is a problem in coarse woods such as oak and ash. The pieces are usually easily dislodged by rubbing a hand or a piece of cloth over the surface. Be careful when using the steel wool near a work-holding device because it can get caught in the jaws or spurs and be pulled out of your hand. This is usually more scary than it is dangerous, however, and the shredded steel wool can be easily unwound from the chuck or drive center.

After sanding and abrading with steel wool, I give a turned piece a last abrading with wood shavings. I collect some of the shavings that have been removed from the workpiece and rub them against the turning wood (Illus. 233). Creating a very fine abrasive action and also considerable heat, this burnishing action makes the wood glow. Use only soft shavings from the workpiece or from an even softer wood. Be careful not to pick up any chips that could score the surface with a spiral groove. Also be careful around any sharp edges because the burnishing action can burn such edges if they are left in contact with the shavings for too long.

Always wear a dust mask while sanding. There are a number of alternatives available with interchangeable filters and various simple devices made of formed, pressed fibres. The simple fibre mask is usually enough to stop the large particulates that even fine sanding creates. The mask must fit snugly on your face, especially for those with beards or moustaches. For some people, the thin elastic of the fibre mask will not make a good seal on the face. The heavier, replaceable filter mask has two heavy elastic bands to fit tightly against the face and will make a better seal. The heavier masks are also recommended for those who are sensitive to one dust in particular or dust in general. They are rated to handle the finer particulates com-

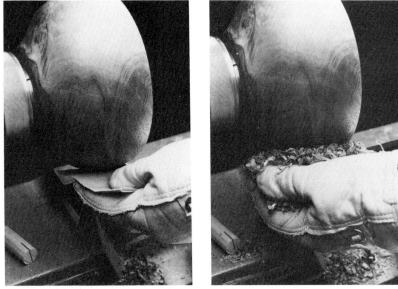

232   233

Illus. 232. Back the sandpaper with a leather glove for small hollows and rounds.

Illus. 233. A final burnishing of the workpiece with soft shavings creates a glowing surface.

mon to finishing and are much safer. Some sanding dusts are considered irritants and will cause sickness. For me, mahogany dust is very irritating, and I wear a dust mask at all times, even when cutting mahogany.

If planning to do a lot of turning, consider a vacuum system a top priority in designing the shop. A powerful cyclone-type separator system, which separates the air from the dust and chips, will catch most of the waste. Disc sanding will send the dust away from the pull of the vacuum, so it is still necessary to wear a mask for this operation.

Finishing

There are three basic reasons for applying a finish to raw wood: to allow the surface to be cleaned and protected against smudges, to seal the wood and control moisture movement in and out of the wood, to enhance grain and color or to cover and hide grain and color. These factors are often combined in a finish that will enhance, protect, and seal. The finishes discussed in this chapter are interior finishes, which lack the high-resin or solids content to withstand the sun's ultraviolet rays and the rain's weathering effects. Paints are generally used for exterior finishes. Heavy oil-based paints protect the wood from water penetration and the resulting bacterial growth that can destroy the wood's structure. This last element is important for glued, thinner pieces, which expand and contract at different rates. A good seal is important to keep these pieces from bursting apart.

Over the years, I have attempted to use the lathe to speed up the finishing process. I have been only moderately successful. There are certain applications and finishes that will benefit from the high speed at which the lathe runs or from the heat and friction of pressing a cloth against a spinning surface. One good example is linseed oil. By heating the oil that is to be applied to the surface, it becomes less viscous and thinner and will penetrate the wood more deeply, making a better seal. Another example is polishing on the lathe. By remounting the piece on the headstock and applying a stationary piece of cloth, it is possible to buff the surface to a high shine.

Nonetheless, I rarely use these methods and for practical reasons. First of all, the lathe area is unsuitable for applying finish. Moving in and around the lathe always creates enough dust to cover a freshly applied finish. Finishing is best done away from the machining area. Applying a liquid finish is also messy. The centrifugal force of the lathe sprays the finish off the wood and onto the lathe, the turner, and the walls. I have also found it difficult to work on pieces that have been remounted because of the difficulty of recentering on the work-holding device. Bowls are more difficult to recenter because after the waste has been removed from the hollow form, the vessel invariably closes in slightly. This, combined with centrifugal force flexing the thin walls of a bowl, makes it difficult to contact the surfaces evenly for sanding or polishing. Sanding a finish on the lathe is a sort of overkill. With the lathe moving at a relatively high speed, the slightest amount of pressure from the sandpaper can easily sand through the finish and expose the raw wood again. This is a real inconvenience when the wood has been stained prior to the addition of another finish.

The following finishes will provide a simple nontechnical overview of available materials. An infinite number of combinations of waxes, oils, and varnishes can be used to create a personal formula. Many of these possibilities are thoroughly discussed in wood-finishing books. Try different approaches and finishes. After discovering the one that satisfies both the function and the form of the product for you and your customer, stick with it. Experiment with different woods and with a varying number of coats.

My favorite is a tung oil varnish. It's a durable finish that requires only a few coats and enhances the wood by allowing it to show through clearly. I also add a bit more tung oil to my solution (one part oil to ten parts mix) for light woods and oiticica oil for dark woods to provide a little added toughness. The tung oil varnish that I use is a mixture made by a quality-conscious manufacturer and is consistent from can to can. To finish off the varnished piece I use a synthetic wax. I spread it on in a very thin film and buff the surface immediately after applying. It is resistant to smudges and will not soften with exposure to heat or catch airborne dust particles. This finish complements the decorative ware that I make without masking the beauty of the wood.

Ultimately, the success or failure of every wooden piece depends on the sanding; as I mentioned before, it is difficult to hide poor sanding under layers of finish.

Shellac. Shellac is made from a natural resin, the secretion of the *Laccifer lacca* insect. It is imported from Burma and India in a dry sheet, flake, or button form. Further refining of this orange, brittle material turns it white and powdery. The orange or white dry shellac is then mixed, or "cut," with denatured alcohol to produce the shellac we buy from stores. Orange shellac is used for dark woods and white is used for lighter woods.

Shellac is classified by the number of shellac solids in the mixture; 4- and 2-pound cut shellac are the most common. The proportion of solids to liquid in a 4-pound cut for example is 4 pounds (1.8 kilograms) of dry flake to 1 gallon (3.8 litres) of liquid alcohol. This mixture can be altered for any number of reasons. For instance, manufacturers provide a 4-pound cut for further cutting or to use as a top coat. A 2-pound cut is much lighter and is used as an initial wash coat to seal the surface and provide a mechanical grip for the next coat.

Using a shellac finish is easy. It dries quickly, and additional coats to build up the finish can be added almost immediately. The finish is moisture-resistant and elastic, moving with the wood as it expands and contracts. But shellac is not a tough abrasion-resistant finish, nor is it alcohol-resistant. Because of these failings it has been superseded by tougher lacquers and varnishes. It is satisfactory for decorative pieces but not for furniture that will be subject to abuse.

Padding is another finishing process. Although similar to the French polishing method revered by wood finishers as the ultimate treatment for wood, it is crude and cannot produce the same results. The pad-shellac method requires a piece of lint-free linen at least 12 in. (30.5 cm) square, some 4-pound shellac, denatured alcohol, and linseed oil. Fold the linen into an oval-shaped pad and dip it into the shellac first. Work the mixture into the pad so that it saturates the linen. Next dip this saturated pad into the alcohol. This will thin the mixture and help it flow evenly on the wood. Work the alcohol into the pad in the same way as you worked in the shellac. With the lathe turning and the tool rest moved completely out of the way, press the pad against the turning wood. Keep the pad moving from side to side so that the material won't load up in one place. When the pad runs out of finish reapply the same way as before. The finish will dry almost immediately, so that more coats can be added to build up the body of the finish. You must wait at least 24 hours for the finish to fully cure before the final rubdown.

Shellac in the mixed solution is an extremely perishable substance and must be treated with care to keep it workable. If storing liquid shellac for any length of time, take the mixture out of the metal can and rebottle it in a glass container or some other nonmetallic package. Metal will eventually discolor stored shellac. My preference is for the air evacuation plastic bottles sold in camera stores for storing darkroom chemicals. They are made like accordions, which can be squeezed to force out the air after some of the liquid has been used.

Sanding sealer. Sanding sealer is an excellent initial coating to put on new wood prior to finishing with lacquer or varnish. Specific formulations of sanding sealer are compatible with either lacquer or varnish, but cannot be used interchangeably. A sanding sealer will fill up the pores and level the surface. This works fine on dense woods like maple, but not on open-grain woods like oak. These woods need a paste filler, which will be discussed next.

Sanding sealer can be brushed, wiped, or sprayed on and takes only an hour or so to dry. It can then be sanded smooth easily with a 220-grit paper. If the sealer has properly cured, the sanding will produce a fine white powder. There are no critical sanding instructions to follow, and it is not worth mounting on the lathe again. Only a few minutes are required to dull the surface created by sanding sealer, and then it is ready for the next coat of sealer.

Paste filler. The best way to completely fill the pores of any wood is with a paste wood filler. Paste wood filler is a combination of boiled linseed oil, crushed quartz, and a drier in a thick syrupy paste. It is available as a clear mixture or colored with an oil. Whenever possible use a color darker than the color the wood will be when stained. A finished surface that has been treated with a paste wood filler is well worth the extra time. The beauty of the perfectly smooth surface can be achieved without any great skill and will improve any piece.

To apply a paste filler first be sure that the filler is well mixed. The quartz will settle to the bottom when stored and even while in use will form a sediment on the bottom of the can. Spread the paste with a brush or cloth over the entire piece if it is small, or over a small section of a larger piece. Try to consciously fill every pore and work the paste around without great concern for the direction of the grain. After the gloss of the filler turns to a dull sheen, take a piece of coarse material such as burlap and rub the wood across the grain. Rubbing the wood with the grain may result in pulling out some of the filler. Keep using fresh sections of the burlap to wipe off more and more filler. When all of the surface filler has been removed by this scrubbing, wipe the surface in the direction of the grain with a soft clean cloth. When no more filler is picked up on the cloth, the wiping process is finished. Check the surface by placing an incandescent bulb at a 45° angle to the surface of the wood and search for any unfilled pores. If all is smooth, let it dry at least overnight, although a full day is safer. The filled surface is now ready for the top coat and stain.

Lacquer. Lacquer is a tough finish made of nitrocellulose. It is long lasting and has good resistance to moisture, alcohol, and heat. Spraying lacquer may be the quickest way to seal wood and build up a transparent or colored surface. Spraying is the standard way to apply lacquer in the furniture industry. Successive coats can be added with little drying time in between, and in the hands of a skilled sprayer lacquer can create a smooth surface without much sanding. Lacquer in the hands of a meticulous craftsman can build a deep finish of extreme beauty. Ten or twenty coats can be applied with intermediate sanding to remove dust spots and level the surface. The finish will be thin, slick, and smooth. Lacquers can be high gloss or rubbed to a matt finish. Spraying is the only practical way to apply lacquer. Brushing lacquers are available but are inconvenient to use because they dry slowly and thus require a fairly dust-free environment. In light of the oils and varnishes available today, brushing lacquers aren't worth the trouble.

The tools needed to spray lacquer are the spray gun and compressor. The compressor is a motor attached to a holding tank with oxygen under pressure. This oxygen is transmitted under pressure through a hose to the gun and is mixed with the finish to produce a fine mist, which can be controlled for intensity and spraying angle. The compressor is as expensive as a moderately priced lathe, and is worth owning if a lacquered finish is desired on many pieces. The compressor can also be used for other air-powered tools such as drills and sanders, thus making it an even more versatile addition to the shop.

Again, compared with some of the other finishes available, the apparatus needed to finish with lacquer is definitely not cost effective for the home shop.

Linseed oil. A boiled linseed-oil finish is one of the most basic finishes available for making a durable, waterproof, and heatproof seal in wood. The finish penetrates deeper than shellac, sanding sealer, or lacquer and forms an elastic, tough bond with the wood. Damaged areas can be easily repaired by an application of a little more oil.

The best method of preparing linseed oil is to heat it in a double boiler until thin and less viscous so that it can be absorbed into the wood. The finish can be brushed or wiped on. Overnight drying is recommended. The second and third coats can be abraded with a fine 600-grit, wet or dry sandpaper using some of the oil itself as a lubricant.

Linseed oil stays soft in the wood and moves with it, expanding and contracting with fluctuations in moisture level. On the other hand, this inability to dry makes it impossible to use other surface finishes such as lacquer or shellac over the linseed oil. Of course, there is no real reason to apply a hard finish because the linseed oil can be built up with a number of coats and waxed to resemble a lacquered finish if a high gloss is desired.

Tung oil. Tung oil is the natural extract of the nut of the tung tree (*Aleurites fordii*) and allied species. It is similar to linseed oil in viscosity but it is more durable as a finish. The tung oil that is available today comes primarily from Venezuela. Compared with linseed oil, tung oil dries to a harder film, is twice as moisture-resistant, and is also quicker drying. Tung oil is often a component in varnishes. In combination with thinners and driers it penetrates the wood and hardens within and on it. Pure tung oil can be mixed in differing proportions with turpentine (50% of each is a good combination) for more penetrating ability.

When using tung oil varnish no special precautions are needed. It can be wiped or brushed on. Overnight drying is recommended so that the film can properly cure. Sanding a properly cured finish will produce a white powder. If it is not cured a gummy residue will appear on the sandpaper. The hardened finish can be sanded to remove surface bumps with 4/0 steel wool or one of the fine wet or dry sandpapers such as 400 or 600 grit.

Polyurethane varnish. Polyurethane is a brittle surface finish based more on plastics technology than on natural components. It does not readily move with the expansion and contraction of the wood, and it also buries the wood's natural look beneath a thick gloss. It is, however, much tougher than any of the other finishes and for this reason often favored for furniture destined for abuse. In addition, it is one of the best resistants to liquids. Apply this varnish in a dust-free space and be sure to allow a drying time of five days or so. This is not true for all polyurethanes, of course, but it is for those used by craftsmen who require a high-solids content.

Waxes. The final coating after all other stains and finishes have been applied and rubbed is wax. Wax is an easily renewed finish and will protect the finish below it from dirt and wear. Wax is available as a liquid or paste, clear or colored. The colored waxes are especially worthwhile for darker woods and porous woods that have not been filled with a paste. A light wax can accumulate in the pores of such wood and turn white when it becomes hard.

Most waxes are manufactured from a combination of beeswax, a by-product of honey making; carnauba wax, an extract of the Brazilian palm tree; and turpentine. It is carnauba wax that gives the mixture its hardness and durability. My current favorite among the waxes is not made of any natural materials at all. It is a synthetic, microcrystalline wax. As such, it is not affected by heat, will not soften after application, nor will it pick up airborne dust particles. It is applied very thinly and can then be buffed immediately.

Illus. 234. When turned joinery is separated, simple socket-and-tenon joints are revealed. See also Illus. 235.

VIII · Adhesives and Clamping

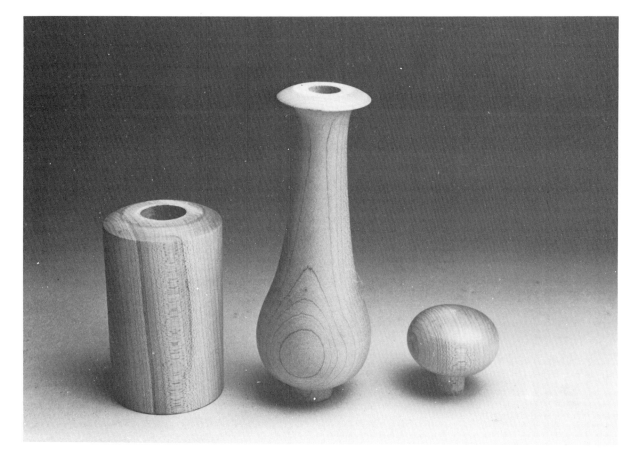

*A*dhesives are used to make permanent bonds between mated pieces of wood. An example of turned joinery is the traditional four-poster bed. The most practical way to make a 5-ft. (152.4-cm) bedpost is to make it in segments. If the full length were used, it would require a correspondingly long lathe bed and two or three steady rests along the workpiece to prevent whipping. By reducing the larger post to more manageable sections, a smaller lathe can be used and the possibility of whipping is greatly reduced.

Woodturning Joints

The most logical location for the glue joints is at a point of decoration. Positioning the glue line to one side of a large bead (Illus. 234 and 235) will make the line invisible to all but the most curious viewer. The joint used, the simple socket and tenon, is one of the oldest in furniture making. The cylindrical tenon end fits into the matching cylindrical socket. The same type of joint is used to join legs to chair seats, legs to stretchers, and handles to mallet heads. Other turned furniture parts also use standard cabinetmaking joints, such as the mortice and tenon, in their construction. In many cases, it is wise to cut the joint before turning the piece because the spindle ends may not be exactly square after turning. Another method of joining two turned pieces is with a larger version of the socket-and-tenon joint in which a wider but shorter stub fits into a shallow recess. The two broad surfaces that are joined are made up of face grain against face grain, and form the best bond of all. Naturally, a tight fit will make a good joint. When inlaying a thinner piece of wood or veneer into a recess on a wooden blank, it is often best to taper the thin piece so that the glue line will be invisible (Illus. 236). This may be risky because the turning operation can remove so much of the wood that the glue line and tapered gap are exposed below the surface. Light cuts must be taken to avoid this.

When making matching parts to be bonded, work slowly and carefully. Check the accuracy of the sections to be mated with a

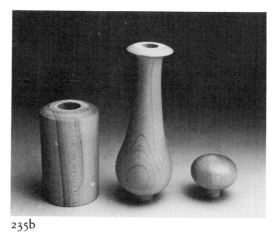

Illus. 235a,b. Turned joinery for a large spindle. Positioning the glue line to the side of a large bead makes the line invisible. Simple socket-and-tenon joints are revealed when the joints are separated.

Illus. 236. Claro walnut bowl with rosewood inlay.

235a

235b

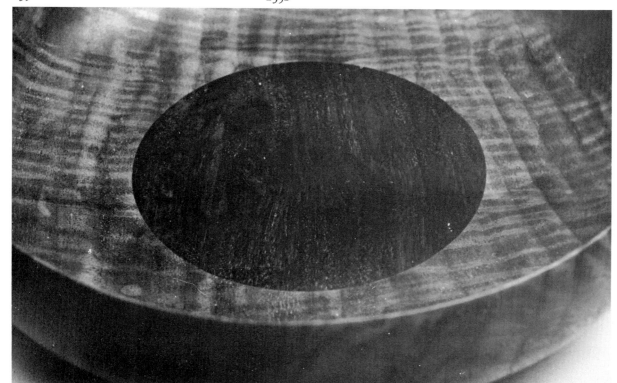

236

straightedge and a square, and stop the lathe often to test-fit the parts. Never sand the mated parts because the rough wood makes a better gluing surface and because it is easy to remove too much, resulting in a sloppy fit. Carelessness is always the reason for a poor fit. A poorly fit socket-and-tenon joint can be repaired by sawing down the center of the tenon and fitting a tapered wedge into the resulting cut (Illus. 237). As the tenon is tightened into the socket, the wedge is pushed deeper into the cut thereby spreading the size of the tenon within the socket. The wedge is not necessary unless the fit is sloppy because water-based glues are absorbed into the wood parts that swell to make the fit even tighter than is apparent when testing the dry joint.

One last point about bonding turned pieces is the gluing itself. It is important to keep the glue runout to an absolute minimum while still coating the mated pieces adequately. Glue runout can be a real hassle on turnings because of the difficulty in removing dried glue from deep decorative cuts. The easiest way to clean off the runout is with a damp rag. Wipe off all glue that runs out after the clamps have been tightened to their limit. Another safe way to protect the

Illus. 237. (a) *To repair a poorly fitting socket-and-tenon joint, saw down the center of the tenon and fit a tapered wedge into it.* (b) *This cut-away view shows the position of the wedge in the tenon.*

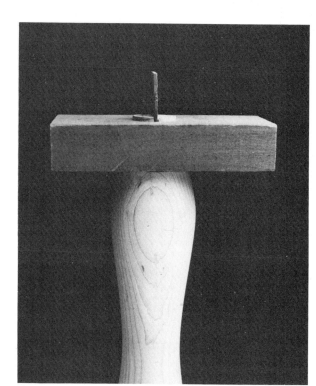

237a

237b

surrounding surfaces from dripping glue is to wax them with ordinary paste wax. The glue dries on the wax and can later be peeled off, and the wax can then be stripped off with turpentine.

Adhesives

The glues discussed below represent the most common glues used by woodturners. They are designed to bond wood to wood and are found in most hardware stores. In addition, there are more than 50 varieties of glue designed for highly specific purposes. See the adhesives section in the *Thomas Register of American Manufacturers* (Thomas Publishing Co., New York, yearly) for laboratories that make customized mixtures.

Naturally, all of these glues require wood surfaces that are clean and free of any trace of finish. It may be necessary, when gluing two surfaces that have been stripped of an old finish, to neutralize the wood of any trace of the wax often used in today's chemical strippers. Gluing highly resinous woods may be difficult because an accumulation of resin on the surface prohibits penetration of the glue. To remove any traces of this resin wipe the surface with a thinner such as mineral spirits or lacquer thinner.

Interior-use adhesives. In the past, white glue was the most popular adhesive. It can be worked and will cure in temperatures as low as 50 °F (10 °C); required clamping time is about one hour; and the glue line is invisible. But it has recently fallen out of favor with many woodworkers because its resistance to moisture is very low.

The most popular glue today is yellow glue, also known as aliphatic resin glue. It has more moisture resistance than white glue and is unaffected by normal moisture in the home. Very few yellow-glue failures have been reported. This glue will remain fluid long enough, even in hot summer months, for all mated surfaces to be properly coated. Clamping time is about one hour, after which the piece should be left to dry overnight before further working. Although this is the conservative way to treat the curing glue, some turners put a curing piece back on the lathe and complete the turning after one to one and one-half hours of drying. The pale yellow glue line on a well-made joint will be invisible in the final finished piece. The minimum temperature for applying and curing is 50 °F (10 °C).

Both white and yellow glues are ready to apply when purchased. They have a water base and as such can be diluted with more water either to make the application easier or to slow down the drying process. In most situations this advantage is meaningless because the glue must be used full strength for maximum holding power.

Exterior-use adhesives. The formaldehyde glues have gained favor among woodworkers for glued joints that will be in intermittent or continuous contact with moisture. The best blend for moisture resistance is the resorcinol-formaldehyde compound, which is available as a two-part solution. Liquid must be mixed with powder to the proper consistency or the glue will barely work. The temperature for working with this glue is in the 70°F (21°C) range, and over three hours are needed for the glue to cure under clamping pressure. There are no shortcuts when working with this glue, and failure of the bond is always possible if the glue is improperly mixed or if clamping pressure is unequal on the glue line. When dry, the glue line is red.

Urea-formaldehyde glue requires much less clamping time, only 20 minutes, but moisture resistance is a bit lower than with resorcinol glue. Many turners, however, use urea-formaldehyde as a general-purpose glue because it takes longer to dry and is more moisture resistant than yellow glue. Before using, add the powdery mix supplied to tap water until the proper consistency is reached. Working and curing temperature must be in the 70°F (21°C) range for the cure to be successful. The resulting glue line is tan.

The final exterior grade glue to consider is the filled epoxy type. It has excellent moisture resistance and can still cure properly when worked as low as 0°F (−18°C). The glue is made by mixing two liquids, glue and hardener, together in the right proportions. The high-solids content is helpful in filling any voids that may be present in the joint.

Storage. Both white and yellow glues are freezable and can be used after thawing. The formaldehyde glues, however, will be significantly weakened by freezing and must be stored in a warm dry spot. Buy these glues in amounts that will be used quickly so that if they get ruined only a small amount will perish.

Clamping

The best clamp of all is the tight-fitting joint. An outside mechanical clamp is also needed to keep the joint together should it try to separate. One way turners have kept joints together in the past is by using the saw kerf and the wedge. As mentioned earlier, by sawing a cut down the center of a tenon and hammering a wedge into it, you enable the tenon to spread in the socket. The basic cabinetmaker's kit of hand screws, bar clamps, and deep engagement clamps (Illus. 238) is also used for applying turned parts to other furniture parts. Band clamps are also useful for tightening together the undercarriage of turned elements on a chair (Illus. 239). Always use more clamps than you think are necessary. You usually get only one chance to do it properly.

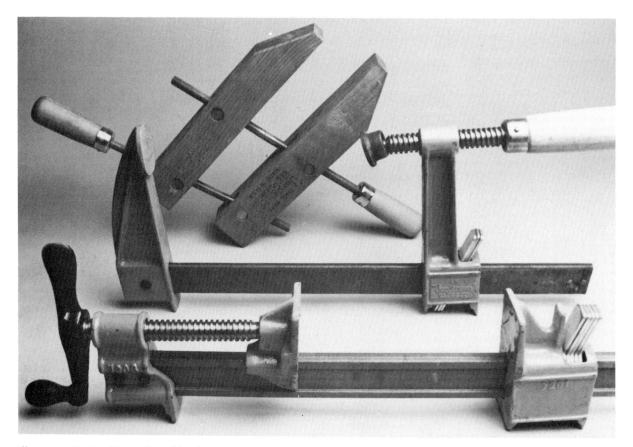

Illus. 238. Basic cabinetmaker's kit of handscrews, above, *bar clamps,* middle, *and deep-engagement clamps,* below.

Illus. 239. Band clamps tighten the undercarriage of the turned elements on this Windsor chair.

Illus. 240. Figure study of red maple burl. See also Illus. 241.

IX · Wood for Turning

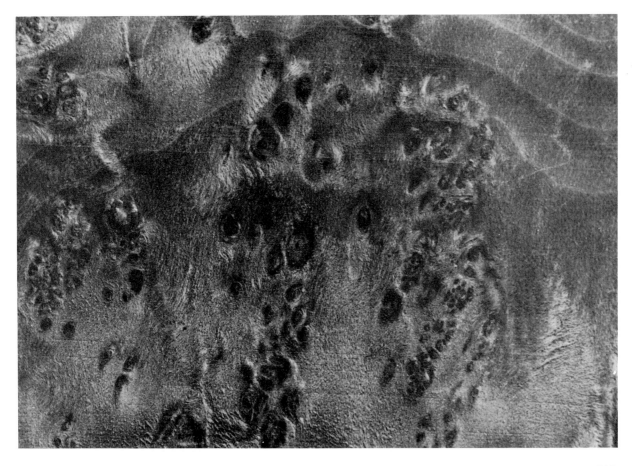

*J*ust as form follows function so choice of wood follows form. For purely decorative objects, the decision is based on figure (grain pattern) and color. For furniture and architectural applications tensile strength is also important.

The following discussion covers many types of wood currently used for turning. Omitted are in-depth discussions concerning the characteristics of the many species of cabinet wood used for turning. This information can fill a book of its own and has. Wood for turning is different from wood used for other kinds of woodworking. It must hold delicate details with little support and in the space of a compact design make a statement in form or lend visual excitement.

Figure and Color

With woodturners concentrating on making decorative accessories today, more than ever before emphasis is placed on the excitement of the wood's grain pattern (Illus. 240–241) or the depth and curiosity of the wood's color. The simple shapes that are in fashion provide broad surfaces for the presentation of the wood. Figure is a function not only of the inherent qualities of the wood, but also of the way the cut is made from the log.

Most wood holds the potential for producing interesting figure. In the furniture industry, maple, for example, is used because of its dense grain, ability to hold details, plain color and figure, and uniform acceptance of colored stains. But maple is an excellent example of a wood that has the capability to produce unusual grain patterns with regularity. Quilted, fiddleback, and curly are names for maple grain patterns that change direction sharply, going from long grain to end grain every inch or so along the length of the plank. Bird's-eye maple is named after the swirling eyes of long grain and end grain that surround central, eyelike knots (Illus. 242). Another aberration common to maple is the burl. Burls are bulbous knobs growing on the outside of trees (Illus. 243). These tree tumors are generally made of interlocking grain with occasional bird's-eyes. The

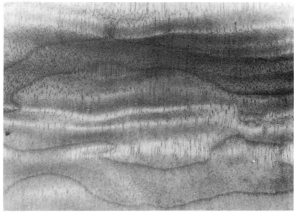

241a

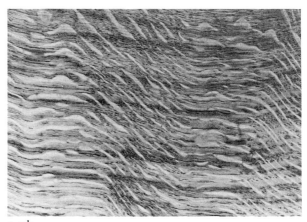

241b

241c

241d

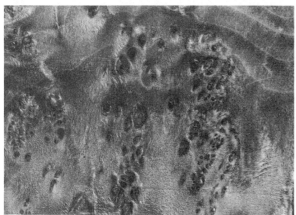

241e

241f

Illus. 241. Figure studies of (a) *curly myrtle,* (b) *English brown oak,* (c) *lacewood,* (d) *straight-grain ash,* (e) *red maple burl, and* (f) *myrtle burl.*

Illus. 242. Bird's-eye maple features swirling eyes composed of long grain and end grain surrounding central eye-like knots.

Illus. 243. Manzanita root burl.

242

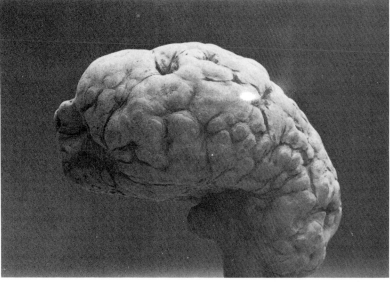

243

burl has always been a popular wood for making bowls because of the interlocking grain, which seems to make it nearly immune to moisture changes from one season to the next. Burls can also grow on underground roots.

The woodturner and the diamond cutter unveil similar surprises when working with their raw material. In both cases, as the waste is removed the beauty of the piece is gradually revealed. For the woodturner discovering great figure depends not only on identifying it but also on careful cutting. Most burl cutting is done with a chain saw. Extracting the right piece of wood for a particular figure depends on making well-placed plunge cuts and crosscuts. When first learning to cut burl wood, it is always best to make broad cuts and to observe the figure as the wood is gradually removed. The only real way to learn about such figured wood is to turn it on the lathe, carefully watching the figure change as the wood is cut away.

Another area for great figure is the crotch of the tree (Illus. 244) where the roots meet the butt. The pattern is shaped like a feather and has the same three-dimensionality as curly or bird's-eye figure. Crotch figure is often found in walnut and is highly prized for thinly cut veneers. The crotch that forms between the butt of the tree and the limbs does not produce this type of figure, and it would be nearly impossible to use such wood because of the competing tensions between the top of the limbs and the underside of the same limb.

Working with figured woods is much easier for the turner than for the cabinetmaker. All of the cabinetmaker's knives and machines must be accurately tuned to produce a smooth even surface without lifting an eye out of a bird's-eye, or tearing out the grain in curly figure. The turner's tools, on the other hand, need only be as sharp as for any other turning. Most of the figures that I have mentioned have consistently hard grain, and no special considerations will need to be taken while cutting them. On some burls, however, pockets of

Illus. 244. Highly prized walnut crotch figure.

fungal decay will appear, and the wood will be deteriorated and soft. Occasionally a tool may dig into and catch in the softer area after making a clean cut in a nearby hard area. For this reason, extra-heavy scrapers were developed. The rock-solid stability of the heavy scraper is not affected by hard or soft grain; it just stays put and shaves away the wood with remarkable control.

Spalting

Spalting can also change figure and color in wood (Illus. 245). Wood left outdoors, close to the ground, and even if covered will absorb moisture and will usually experience fungal activity that spreads following the cells of the tree. The wood, discolored by black or brown zone lines, and the pattern can be very attractive, resembling marble. Spalting occurs in maple and birch with regularity but is not exclusive to them. Setting up a suitable environment for spalting your own wood is easy. It is important to check the wood periodically so that the process can be stopped before the fungus goes too far, and the wood becomes soft and punky. A lot of the wood will not be usable because of unseen cracks and softness on the inside of the block. But what is usable can often be spectacular.

Exotic Color

Color depends on a wood's species and the climatic forces to which it has been subjected. Exotic Asian, South American, and African

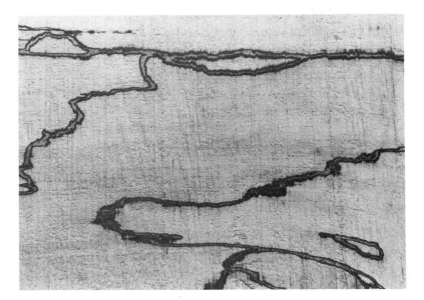

Illus. 245. Fungal activity produces spalting in maple.

hardwoods, such as rosewood, bubinga, and cocobolo, are prized because of their striking, deep color. They have dense grains (Illus. 246) and are highly resinous. Turning highly resinous wood will

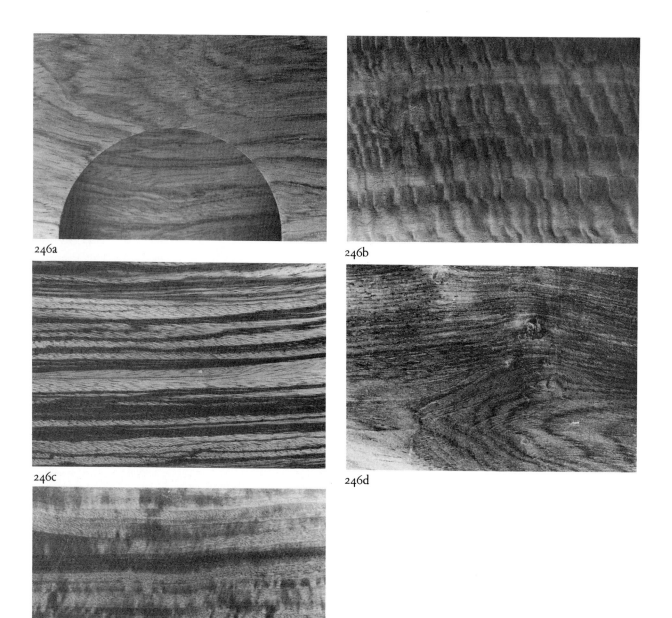

246a

246b

246c

246d

246e

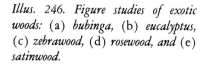

Illus. 246. Figure studies of exotic woods: (a) *bubinga,* (b) *eucalyptus,* (c) *zebrawood,* (d) *rosewood, and* (e) *satinwood.*

dull tools more quickly than turning domestic hardwoods, another good reason to use the more durable high-speed steel. High resin content also enables the wood to take on a reflective sheen when cut properly. A wood like macassar ebony with its jet black and brown, nearly grainless figure is very short-grained and dense. When cut properly it resembles metal more than wood. Such woods cut easily and can take the most delicate detail, although in general they do not cut quickly unless turned while green.

Drying

Discussion among turners often concerns methods of drying wood for turning and the advantages of air versus kiln drying, a reasonable topic because of the thick sections of wood that are often used for bowl or vessel turning. The answer to most questions concerning the turning of thick pieces of wood is usually to turn green wood. This means that the block of wood, its cells still filled with bound water, is mounted on the lathe and most of the interior of the hollow is removed. The key factor in this type of treatment is that the thickness of the walls of the bowl form be the same at every point of the piece. A 1-in. (25-mm) thickness is generally regarded as enough to allow sufficient wood for later refining of the shape (Illus. 247). But if one section of the form is thinner than another, unequal release of the stress in the wood will cause distortion in the form. A

Illus. 247. Green wood is hollowed to a 1-in. (25 mm) thickness and allowed to dry for up to six months prior to the final refining of its shape.

5-in. (12.7-cm) block of wood, which by the old dictum for drying wood would take five years to dry properly, can take six months or less when roughed out first in this way. There is no general rule for the amount of time necessary for wood to reach an equilibrium with the surrounding atmosphere. The key is to periodically check the weight of the wood. When it stops losing weight, then it is probably dry. Woods bought at the lumber yard may have been kiln-dried down to a low moisture content which will rise again considerably during the rainy season.

Occasionally you will encounter wood that behaves erratically and wants to twist out of shape even when treated conservatively and rough-hollowed to a 1-in. (25-mm) thickness for drying. For this type of wood, it is necessary to slow down the drying process even more by putting the roughed-out block in an enclosed container such as a plastic trash bag. This will create a microclimate that will ease the wood into a state of equilibrium, an inexpensive and practical solution to the problem.

Hardwood dealers do stock wood as thick as 4 in. (10.2 cm). The wood is usually kiln-dried at great expense in energy as the bound moisture is driven out of the wood. Most of the wood at the lumber dealer is furniture-grade wood with straight grain and fairly homogeneous color. Interestingly grained wood for the turner is rare but available from specialty dealers. Also, sawmills can be sources because interesting logs appear during their regular cuttings.

If planning to store wood in plank form, be sure that it is under cover and that the ends of the plank are sealed. If the ends are left unsealed, they will be the primary source for the in-and-out flow of moisture, and the result will be deep cracks or checking. Sealing up the end grain will force more of the moisture to move out of the wood through the long grain and drying will be more even. There are commercial applications on the market for sealing the end grain; Chapman Sealtite 60 is one and Mobil Cer-M is another. The same effect is achieved by applying a mixture of yellow glue and water, mixed ten parts water to one part or slightly more of glue. Total prevention of the checking is impossible; the resulting waste is to be expected.

Some woodturners use a paraffinlike substance called polyethylene glycol (PEG) to soak the wood in and to replace the naturally bound water. The mixture is heated in a vat to a specific temperature, and the wood is immersed in it. After a prescribed number of days, the wood is taken out and allowed to dry by evaporation. This is the only way turners can use cross sections of logs or wood that includes deadwood located at the tree's center. Without the PEG the wood would crack and distort after and during the turning process. The only practical finish for wood treated with PEG is a polyurethane finish. This tough plastic finish seals in the heat-softened PEG and keeps it within the wood, because PEG does have a tendency to "bleed" up to the surface when the wood is warm or subjected to direct sunlight.

Structural Strength

When a turning is to be used for an architectural application or in furniture, we must be concerned with its structural integrity. Factors such as shear and tensile strength are important and eliminate all but a few of the softwoods from consideration. When using a turning in an architectural application, consult the *Architectural Graphic Standards* (edited by C. G. Ramsey and H. R. Sleeper, 7th ed. American Institute of Architects, New York, John Wiley & Sons, 1981) for the appropriate graphic standards chart to determine feasibility. The key structural consideration in using turnings in larger pieces is grain straightness. Most structural failures related to turnings indicate improperly selected wood.

Early spindle turners selected straight-grained trees free of twists or other irregularities in the grain along the butt of the tree. The wood was also split out of the tree with a mallet and froe, which separates the wood along the grain lines. Any apparent grain runout problems were identified, and that wood was used for firewood. It is this wood selection process that in the end differentiates the mass-produced piece from the limited-production craftsman-made piece. See Illus. 248 for an example of grain runout on a chair leg. The break occurred at the point of the greatest stress—the fulcrum point where the leg joins the seat. The break was clean because it occurred with the grain, which ran off to the side instead of running the entire length of the leg. Such a break is not really worth repairing when it happens. The only solution is to make a proper leg with straight grain from end to end.

Illus. 248. Grain runout on a chair leg. The break occurred at the point of greatest stress—where the seat joins the leg.

Appendixes

APPENDIX A

Morse Tapers

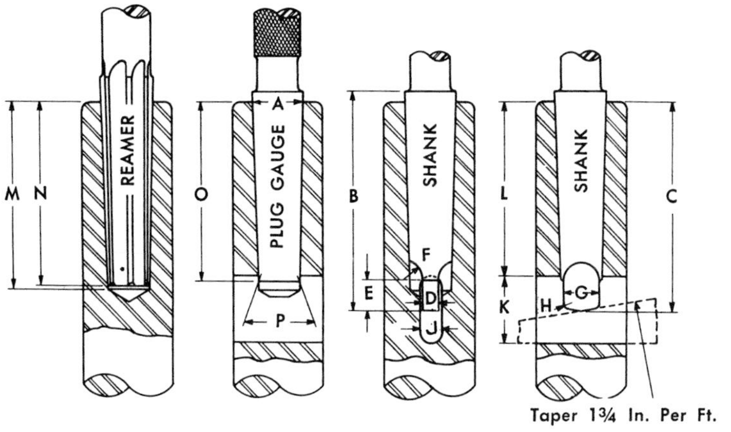

Table Specifications of Morse Tapers

number of taper	diam. of plug at small end	diam. at end of socket	shank: whole length	shank: depth	socket: end of socket to tang slot	socket: depth of drilled hole	socket: depth of reamed hole	socket: standard plug depth	tang: thickness	tang: length	tang: radius	tang: diameter	tang: radius	tang slot: width	tang slot: length	taper per inch	taper per foot
	P	A	B	C	L	M	N	O	D	E	F	G	H	J	K		
0	.25200	.35610	2 11/32	2 7/32	1 15/16	2 1/16	2 1/32	2	.156	1/4	5/32	15/64	3/64	.172	9/16	.052050	.62460
1	.36900	.47500	2 9/16	2 7/16	2 1/16	2 3/16	2 5/32	2 1/8	.203	3/8	3/16	11/32	3/64	.218	3/4	.049882	.59858
2	.57200	.70000	3 1/8	2 15/16	2 1/2	2 21/32	2 39/64	2 9/16	.250	7/16	1/4	17/32	1/16	.266	7/8	.049951	.59941
3	.77800	.93800	3 7/8	3 11/16	3 1/16	3 5/16	3 1/4	3 3/16	.312	9/16	9/32	23/32	5/64	.328	1 3/16	.050196	.60235
4	1.02000	1.23100	4 7/8	4 5/8	3 7/8	4 3/16	4 1/8	4 1/16	.469	5/8	5/16	31/32	3/32	.484	1 1/4	.051938	.62326
4½	1.26600	1.50000	5 3/8	5 1/8	4 5/16	4 5/8	4 9/16	4 1/2	.562	11/16	3/8	1 13/64	1/8	.578	1 3/8	.052000	.62400
5	1.47500	1.74800	6 1/8	5 7/8	4 15/16	5 5/16	5 1/4	5 3/16	.625	3/4	3/8	1 13/32	1/8	.656	1 1/2	.052626	.63151
6	2.11600	2.49400	8 9/16	8 1/4	7	7 13/32	7 21/16	7 1/4	.750	1 1/8	1/2	2	5/32	.781	1 3/4	.052138	.62565
7	2.75000	3.27000	11 5/8	11 1/4	9 1/2	10 5/32	10 5/64	10	1.125	1 3/8	3/4	2 5/8	3/16	1.156	2 5/8	.052000	.62400

Reprinted from *The Machinist's Practical Guide,* Morse Cutting Tools Division of Gulf & Western Manufacturing Co., New Bedford, Mass., 1979, pages 44–45.

APPENDIX B

Band Saw Blade Widths and Their Corresponding Radii

Blade Width	Radius
½ in. (13 mm)	2½ in. (64 mm)
⅜ in. (10 mm)	1¼ in. (32 mm)
¼ in. (6 mm)	⅝ in. (16 mm)
3/16 in. (5 mm)	⅜ in. (10 mm)
⅛ in. (3 mm)	7/32 in. (5 mm)

APPENDIX C

Lumber Sizes and Their Corresponding Lathe Speeds

There are different points of view regarding lathe speeds. Some turners favor the slow speeds of a treadle lathe. Others favor cranking up the speed as high as possible for the size of the wood to be turned. Safety and efficiency for the turner are of primary importance. Of secondary importance is matching the revolutions of the workpiece to the cutting action of the tool.

For years I used 1700 r.p.m. for about 90% of the turning I did, which included cutting, scraping, and sanding. As my techniques matured, I found that this moderate speed was too slow and restrictive. Using the highest speeds took some bravado initially, but I found them to be better suited to fast cutting, which I came to prefer and which I am now more comfortable with.

There is a relationship between the rotation speed and the rate of manual or automatic feed of the cutting tool into the wood. This speed and rate of feed are similar to those for planks and the revolving circular saw blade.

Some turners also prefer high speeds for sanding operations. I have found that high speeds for this work often defeat the purpose and result in the burning or burnishing of the worn abrasive. For sanding I can produce good results using the same speed that I used for cutting or scraping. This also holds true for sanding with a disc sander.

The following chart of lumber sizes and their corresponding lathe speeds is reprinted here, courtesy of Delta International Machinery Corp., Pittsburgh, Penn.

Lumber Size (diameter)	Lathe Speed (r.p.m.)
Under 2 in. (51 mm)	2400–2800
2–4 in. (51–102 mm)	1800–2400
4–6 in. (10.2–15.2 cm)	1200–1800
6–8 in. (15.2–20.3 cm)	800–1200
8–10 in. (20.3–25.4 cm)	600–800
Over 10 in. (25.4 cm)	300–600

APPENDIX D

Metric Equivalency Chart

MM—MILLIMETRES   CM—CENTIMETRES

Inches to millimetres and centimetres

INCHES	MM	CM	INCHES	CM	INCHES	CM
⅛	3	0.3	9	22.9	30	76.2
¼	6	0.6	10	25.4	31	78.7
⅜	10	1.0	11	27.9	32	81.3
½	13	1.3	12	30.5	33	83.8
⅝	16	1.6	13	33.0	34	86.4
¾·	19	1.9	14	35.6	35	88.9
⅞	22	2.2	15	38.1	36	91.4
1	25	2.5	16	40.6	37	94.0
1¼	32	3.2	17	43.2	38	96.5
1½	38	3.8	18	45.7	39	99.1
1¾	44	4.4	19	48.3	40	101.6
2	51	5.1	20	50.8	41	104.1
2½	64	6.4	21	53.3	42	106.7
3	76	7.6	22	55.9	43	109.2
3½	89	8.9	23	58.4	44	111.8
4	102	10.2	24	61.0	45	114.3
4½	114	11.4	25	63.5	46	116.8
5	127	12.7	26	66.0	47	119.4
6	152	15.2	27	68.6	48	121.9
7	178	17.8	28	71.1	49	124.5
8	203	20.3	29	73.7	50	127.0

Index

(Numbers in italics refer to illustrations.)